The Aroma Freedom
Technique
Second Edition

Using Essential Oils to Transform Your Emotions and Realize Your Heart's Desire

Dr. Benjamin Perkus
Licensed Psychologist

Aroma Freedom International
Binghamton, NY
USA

Connect on Facebook at facebook.com/aromafreedom

You may reach Dr. Perkus at www.drperkus.com

The Aroma Freedom Technique: Using Essential Oils to Transform Your Emotions and Realize Your Heart's Desire – Second Edition/ Dr. Benjamin Perkus

ISBN 978-0-9976494-2-0

Disclaimer:

The information contained in this book is for educational purposes only. The author is not rendering professional advice or services to the individual reader. If you are experiencing emotional or physical distress, please consult the appropriate medical provider. Nothing herein should be construed as an attempt to diagnose or treat any medical condition. Although unlikely, if you experience any negative or allergic reactions to the essential oils, please discontinue use and seek medical attention.

This book is dedicated to:

My wife and partner Elaine for inspiring and challenging me to be my best self every day and for insisting on quality and excellence at every stage of this project.

My daughter Eyana Rose who will inherit a world that is hopefully more awake, aware, conscious due to the understanding we now have about how to live with emotional freedom, joy, and love.

Dr. Gary Young, who has been a pioneer in the re-introduction of essential oils to the world and who has contributed so much to the understanding of essential oil farming, distillation, science, and use. Without his groundbreaking work and uniquely inspired blends this technique could not have been created.

My students and colleagues who have embraced The Aroma Freedom Technique and have worked to transform their own lives and the lives of countless others. You have helped to create a wonderfully supportive environment to nurture and guide the outgrowth of AFT into the world. Your commitment and creativity brings this work to new places every day!

Finally, to all the people who are seeking better ways to find emotional balance and purpose in life, and who are embracing a new paradigm of self-responsibility and consciousness – this book is for you.

Table of Contents

A Note on Required Training:

You are encouraged to try this technique on yourself, family, and friends simply using what you learn in this book. However, if you would like to integrate AFT into any kind of clinical work (psychotherapy, massage, etc.), or if you want to charge for sessions or to teach AFT for commercial gain, then you must become a Certified AFT Practitioner.

More information about becoming a Certified AFT Practitioner can be found at www.drperkus.com.

Additionally, you can request Dr. Perkus to speak to your group or organization through the same portal.

Preface to the Second Edition

A mother takes her two teenage children through a brief Aroma Freedom Technique (AFT) process in the evening and they release the painful memories they have been carrying. They now feel hopeful and positive about going to school the next day.

A Psychologist uses AFT on herself to release long-held feelings of inadequacy, and grows closer to her husband.

A former manager of a nonprofit agency discovers AFT and is so moved by her personal experiences that she decides to become an AFT instructor and to devote her time to helping others in business have similar breakthroughs.

A sales team leader uses AFT to help her team become more confident in their vision and, months later, they are all still more focused and productive than ever.

A practitioner with an 8-year history of terror when seeing carpenter ants releases this fear with one self-guided AFT session and decides to rededicate her entire practice to AFT.

 A pastor releases a longstanding craving for caffeine in a simple, ten-minute session.

A man who had always felt angry during his long commute was able to completely shift his attitude in one AFT session and is now making changes in other areas of his life.

The owner of a large Psychology practice learns AFT and integrates it into her work with some of her most difficult clients. It makes such a difference she decides to have her whole team of therapists trained in the technique.

It has been almost a year since the first edition of *The Aroma Freedom Technique* came out. In that time, we have seen thousands of lives transformed by learning how pure essential oils, when inhaled in the right combination and in the proper order, can release the negative thoughts, feelings, and memories that hold people back from pursuing their dreams.

This success forces us to re-think many of our assumptions about how long it takes to rebound from the doubts, fears, and worries that plague so many people. It also puts into the hands of every person the means to identify and release subconscious beliefs that are holding them back. What impact does this have in everyday life?

For myself, this technique allowed me to finally write the book I had been waiting 20 years to write, and to teach others how to do what they have been waiting to do.

When people are empowered to pick themselves up again after disappointment, or to find clarity when they are confused, or to embrace the future rather than clinging to the past, they are much more productive, energized, and happy. The impact this can potentially have on society is enormous.

There will always be a need for trained professional counselors when people are lost and needing direction and advice. But using the simple tool of AFT, either on oneself or on a client, brings a speed and completeness to the process that opens a whole new world of possibilities for success and freedom.

Here is a quote from one of our certified practitioners about her AFT journey:

"I have been an avid oil user for 7 years, and I have been using oils specifically for emotions and emotional release for many of those years. So I did not think that there would be a technique out there that would bring about any significant differences beyond those I already was seeing.

I was wrong. When I finally decided to give AFT a try, I was amazed at how targeted and specific I could get in dealing with emotions, blocks, and memories. I have found so much freedom in SO many areas of my life in just the few months I have been practicing it! Even my beliefs (and my ability TO believe) have changed drastically. I feel I am so much more open minded, so much more able to accept new ideas or dream new dreams for myself and my business and family! Wow, I didn't even realize the prison that my mind was holding me in!

I have done only a few sessions (individual and group), and already been amazed to see them opening their minds to so many new things. I wish I could share AFT with every single person on my team, and especially every leader, so they can move through their own issues faster and see the successes they so desperately want and need!

My biggest plan is to continue to expose my leaders to this technique, so they can use it for their life and business, and share it with their teams!"

Jolin Housewright, Frisco, TX

Why do people love AFT?

1) It is simple. Easily learned and taught, it does not require years of study to master.
2) It can be done by anyone. AFT is designed to help people make breakthroughs in their everyday life.
3) It feels good! By the end of a session, people feel excited and empowered to pursue their dreams and goals.

AFT was created to be used <u>only</u> with Young Living Essential Oils. When you deeply inhale an essential oil, it needs to be pure and of the highest quality. The brain is a very sensitive organ and it is important to make sure you are not inhaling oils that may have solvents, synthetic constituents, or pesticides. Young Living's Seed to Seal Process ensures that what you are smelling is only the purest oil, properly cultivated, distilled, tested, and bottled.

Additionally, the blends created by Dr. Gary Young that are used in AFT were specifically designed to transform and release negative emotions, and place you into a positive, life-affirming attitude.

Young Living Essential Oils are marketed through a network of independent distributors who teach the people who they enroll how to use the oils and where to find additional resources. Relationships are very important in this process. If someone you know has introduced you to Young Living Essential Oils or to this book, please work with them to get the oils you need for this process. If you do not have a relationship with anyone yet in Young Living, you can find the oils you need for AFT at **www.drperkus.com** – we will show you how to use the oils for emotional balance as well as a multitude of household and wellness uses. We have been using Young Living Essential Oils in our family for over 15 years and we love how they support us in all areas of our life.

It is my hope that, as AFT continues to grow, people will cease being locked in the fears, doubts and worries that plague them, but instead use the process to regain the joy, openness, and creativity that is their birthright. Now that we understand where our inner resistance comes from and how to release it, we can break through to a more abundant life for everyone.

Dr. Benjamin Perkus
Sandy, Utah
May 2017

Preface to the First Edition

Do you like going fast?

I did.

I was 15 years old, a senior in high school. This was the first year that I was on the track team. I was never a great athlete but I was slender and enthusiastic. It was our first meet, and I was set to run in the 1-mile track race. When the starting gun went off, I took off running as fast as I could. To everyone's surprise, I had shot out ahead of the pack. My team was cheering me on, as I continued to be ahead of everyone after half a mile.

Then, at about the three-quarter mile mark, I hit the wall. My legs stopped carrying me as fast as they had been. Even though my mind wanted me to keep going fast, my legs had run out of gas. To my dismay, the other runners who had been behind me now started passing me. I tried to push harder but it seemed like there was just no more speed that I could muster. I finished 5th or 6th. I was dismayed that my body had let me down.

At the time, I did not understand why my body responded that way. I now know what happened – I had never run the mile race before and my pace was too fast – I burned out. Also, as a new runner I had not built up glycogen reserves in my muscles – the fuel that muscles can burn when they run out of sugar. Back then, however, all I knew was that I had failed on that day.

This event from my life 30+ years ago was a mildly painful experience by most standards – not terribly traumatic, certainly not bad enough to have a lasting impact on a person, or so I thought. After that race, I recovered, finished the track season, got on with my life, and never thought much more about it, until recently…

Just the other day I was part way through a major editing session, working to finish this very book you are now reading. I had set a tight timeline to finish the book, because like many people, I tend to get things done better when I am sprinting towards a deadline. Yet something strange was happening – I felt like I was hitting some sort of wall – my brain wouldn't work anymore and I felt I had no choice but to stop what I was doing and take a break.

Thankfully, I had enough presence of mind to realize that perhaps there was a deeper component to my fatigue. I took myself through the process of what I have come to call the Aroma Freedom Technique, the steps of which you will learn in this book. In less than 10 minutes, I had identified a thought - "I am not strong enough," a feeling

– "discouragement," and the memory of my running failure as a teenager that had apparently become triggered by my current *sprint* towards the end of my writing project.

So, I pulled out my trusty essential oils, and smelled them as I thought of the newly awakened memory complex. Sure enough, after about 30 seconds the emotional charge to the memory had weakened, and new, empowering beliefs began to spring forth in my mind. I pictured myself running through the finish line, successful and proud. Once my emotional energy shifted through this process, it was fascinating to see how quickly my brain turned back on and I was ready to go "back to work." The result is the book you now hold in your hands.

*   *   *

This is a book about enabling you to be your best self, and allowing you to cross the finish line of your choosing. We all have goals and dreams that spring from our heart, and my desire is to help you achieve those goals and dreams by showing you how to overcome the *inner resistance* that may be stopping you.

To be happy you need to live a life of purpose. Happiness is not a goal in and of itself; it is a side-effect of doing what you are meant to do in this life. It involves giving your talents and abilities to a cause or a purpose that takes you beyond yourself. People who are living a purpose-filled life are not bothered by all of the little things that can go wrong in a day – they are too focused on their mission to worry about such things.

The trouble is, most people have become disconnected

from their dreams because, in the process of adjusting to life, they have lost themselves or they have lost their belief that they *could* reach their dreams. When I was 15 I had developed a belief that I was not strong enough to cross the finish line. When people don't believe in themselves, they lose that spark of curiosity, enthusiasm, and engagement that they may have once had.

In this book I will describe how this whole process happens, and, more importantly, how to get it back. I will show you how you can use your sense of *smell*, your most primitive and emotionally potent sense, to re-wire your brain in the direction of alignment with your dreams.

Based on years of clinical practice, I created the Aroma Freedom Technique (AFT) as a process for anyone to use to identify and clear the way for their goals and dreams to manifest. Mental Health Professionals will find AFT to be a valuable tool to help clients move more quickly and deeply through painful memories, and into emotional freedom.

The restrictions we feel in life are a result of limiting beliefs, attitudes, and memories that we have developed in the process of growing. You will see how traumatic events can cloud our ability to approach life in an open way. Even mildly upsetting events can shape our future attitudes significantly.

Aroma, specifically that of a pure essential oil, has the power to soften the emotionally charged memories and modify our resulting attitudes. The Aroma Freedom

Technique is a series of easy-to-follow steps that will allow you to break free from the limits you have imposed on yourself.

The steps are arranged in a specific order for a good reason, based on countless hours of clinical practice and observation about what gets people stuck and how to get them free, so I encourage you to learn them in order. Once you have mastered the basics, you can play with the technique and find your own variations. By following these steps, you will have a gentle and powerful way to get yourself "unstuck" and back in motion in the direction of your dreams.

May, 2016
Charlottesville, VA

Part 1: Scent, Memory and Emotion

Introduction

We set goals and then don't achieve them. We know we should do things and then don't do them. Why? Where does all this *inner resistance* come from? Why is it so common for people to feel unable to do the things that they know that they want to do and should do? Why are people constantly fighting with themselves when it comes to reaching their goals? I will give you a hint – *the answer is closer than you think.*

To find out, let's do an experiment. Permit me to ask you a few questions. As I do, notice your response:

Do you deserve to be happy?

Are you confident you can get what you want in life?

Do you expect good things to happen in your life?

Do you feel loved and appreciated by those around you?

Are you satisfied in your career?

Do you feel financially secure?

Do you enjoy vigor and vitality?

If you answered "yes" to all of these questions and there was no inner voice raising objections, congratulations! You can put this book down now and go on with your life.

If you are like most people, however, at some point you will have heard an inner voice inside that said some statements like:

"Yeah, right."

"I wish."

"This book is stupid. Nobody can have all of those things."

"Other people can have those things, but my situation is different."

"I could have that if it wasn't for _____ (spouse/boss/parent/child/co-worker)

"What is this, some kind of fairy tale?"

"Give me a break."

> Pay attention to these inner objections.
> They are here for a reason. They are here
> to protect you.
>
> The trouble is, they are trying to protect you
> from a situation that no longer exists.

The fact is, we have *all* experienced pain, loss, sadness, anger, frustration etc. in our lives at some earlier time.

And when we did, we formed beliefs, thoughts, and attitudes to protect us from feeling these unpleasant things in the future.

These are the objections that you heard your inner voice saying when you read some statements about things most of us really want. These objections (the combination of which is a major component of what has been called the *ego*) are trying to convince you not to do something that has caused pain in the past. Yet this voice is also stopping you from doing or being something that you really want to do or be.

The story of Sally is a good illustration of the kind of changes that frequently occur with the Aroma Freedom Technique:

Sally came to me because she just didn't feel, as she put it, "right." Although normally a positive, upbeat person, her friends were telling her that she seemed to be acting more negative, pessimistic, and downcast lately. She was seeing only the downside of every situation, and was overly focused on the fearful and dangerous possibilities of life instead of the joy and beauty that she used to see.

She agreed to try a round of the Aroma Freedom Technique, and within about ten minutes her mood started to shift. We identified where she had gotten stuck, and more importantly, we were able to get her on track again.

I used the step-by-step process of AFT outlined in part 2 of this book. First, she needed to set a goal. She said that she would like to get back to how she used to be: "confident, optimistic, and positive." I had her identify what the little voice in her head said to her when she stated this intention. "That's a joke" was her inner reply. We now focused on her feelings when she heard that inner voice. She felt confused because she didn't want to lie to herself. She didn't want to *pretend* that she was ok when really she wasn't.

Through the AFT process she was brought to a memory of a time about 20 years previously when a family member had tragically died and her boyfriend was showing no empathy at all. She had been so devastated by his lack of support that she had just shut down and had become unexpressive. It had been too much for her to process – she was in deep grief and shock, and her boyfriend, whom she *thought* was a good match for her, was becoming angry and abusive. She remembered trying to go on with her life – going to work, etc. – but inside she was shaken to the core.

I had her focus on that memory as I put three drops of essential oil in her palm. She smelled the oil and breathed it into the memory. As she did this, some tears came and she just released them for a few seconds. I had her smell one more drop of a different oil to help her to release more deeply. After another minute her face began to brighten up and her breathing became more regular.

She reported that the memory had become more "far away" and she no longer was as bothered by the memory from 20 years ago. It was as if the memory, which just seconds earlier seemed so painful and real, now receded to its proper place as a part of her history.

When we went back to the original statement about being confident, optimistic, and positive, she smiled. She said that she felt hopeful and optimistic again – not perfect, but like a ray of light was shining through. She realized that the current stressors in her life – financial uncertainty and moving to a new city – had triggered an early memory that had just been overwhelming.

I helped her to create an affirmation that said "I am grounded, optimistic, and radiant." She liked the concept of being optimistic while still grounded in reality, and also that she could choose to be radiant no matter what was happening in her life. I told her to say this statement 3 times, morning and night. After the session, she felt lighter and her husband said that her energy had shifted and he felt that she was becoming brighter again.

The AFT process is a simple tool for identifying and transforming negative emotional traces that may be interfering with our current life goals and intentions. It is not a replacement for psychotherapy, nor a tool that will solve all of life's problems. Rather, it is meant to be used as a way to get a person's emotional energy flowing in a positive direction, towards growth and expansion rather than contracting in fear, doubt, and paralysis.

It can be used as an excellent aid to the psychotherapeutic process, incorporated into various forms of healing work, or even used daily as a way to make sure that we are aligned with our goals. It complements our work towards our goals, but it does not replace that work. If I want to build a house, I can use the AFT process to make sure my energy is aligned with that process but I still have to go through all of the other phases of housebuilding.

One of the central insights of Psychology over the last 100+ years is that early experiences shape our beliefs and attitudes, and that these beliefs influence how we approach our later life. With that being said, there are now dozens of types of therapy aimed at managing our emotions or changing our behaviors.

> This book describes a method that draws upon many of the existing therapeutic techniques, but combines them with essential oils in an entirely new way.

The method is designed to be very flexible and to be used by individuals at home as well as by people in the helping professions.

It aims to address the kinds of problems that people seek help for in the first place, namely, how to find satisfaction in love, work, health, family, recreation, etc.

I believe that we are all born with not only the desire to be happy and fulfilled, but the means by which we can create satisfaction in our lives. Life is a continual process of growth, as long as we keep our emotional energy moving.

But I am getting ahead of myself. Many people ask me:

> "Can essential oils *really* help with emotional balancing?"

I get this type of question a lot when I tell people that I am a Clinical Psychologist and that I use essential oils in my practice.

The fact is, I was never taught about aromatherapy in my Ph.D. program. Even after I began my practice and I was exploring the new world of energy psychology that was starting to gain attention in the 1990's, I never heard of aromatherapy being used in a clinical setting. The popular perception was that aromatherapy is something that could be mildly relaxing or gently uplifting (which it is), but that it would be no match for the kinds of emotional problems that people really struggle with.

Even after I was introduced to essential oils in 2001, it was unclear to me that they could reach deeply enough into the psyche to be all that useful in clinical practice or even for personal transformational work.

Now, I think differently.

You are probably reading this book because you value personal growth and development. You may know someone who is having trouble maintaining emotional balance. Or you may be a mental health professional looking for ways to help your clients. In any of these cases you will find here a simple yet powerful technique for using awareness combined with essential oils to deeply process and release emotional reaction patterns that are no longer useful. Do not be deceived by its apparent simplicity. Each step of the process is built upon psychological principles that are based upon how human beings function emotionally. Emerging brain science is confirming these principles and allowing for greater precision in how we can regain emotional freedom.

The technique described in this book was first developed as a method to help people regain emotional balance after they had undergone stressful events and were still bothered by them. When we experience an upsetting, fearful or very intense event, we may be bothered afterwards by the memory of the event and can't seem to regain our composure, even though we try to put it out of our minds. When I had people focus on the various components of the memory complex – namely, the image, feeling, bodily sensation, and negative thoughts – and then smell specific essential oils, the image seemed to "break apart" or recede into the distance and not seem so intense or upsetting.

A breakthrough came when I discovered that if I asked a person a set of questions in a specific order, they could stumble upon memories that were linked to their current problems even though they may never have associated these memories with the current situation. This is because the amygdala and hippocampus (parts of the brain) link together memories based on common feeling rather than any cognitive context.

Although this method seems simple, it builds upon the work of many pioneers in the field of Psychology, including Eugene Gendlin's *Focusing*, Carl Jung's *Active Imagination*, Aaron Beck's *Cognitive Psychology*, Freud's *Memory Regression*, Fritz Perls' *Gestalt* processes, Francine Shapiro's *Eye Movement Desensitization Reprocessing (EMDR)*, and of course many others too numerous to mention.

When I learned about Dr. Gary Young's re-discovery of essential oil use for emotional clearing (which he found in studying the practices of ancient Egyptians), I recognized a missing piece that would allow these processes to work more quickly and deeply due to fact that the amygdala responds instantaneously to the sense of smell.

In using essential oils to assist with processing of stressful memories, I was struck by how there seemed to be a spontaneous re-alignment of images, feelings, and belief systems as people smelled the oils while in a particular phase of the release process. There seems to be a deep connection between the sense of smell and memory, and we were somehow changing the meaning of these memories by introducing the oils at the right time.

Most people can relate to the experience of smelling

something that immediately conjures up a memory, sometimes from long ago, complete with details and often strong feelings. Smelling fresh baked bread may remind us of our grandmother's kitchen, or the smell of a mechanic's garage may remind us of watching our father fix cars in the driveway. We feel literally transported to those previous times, immediately and without warning. This experience is so well known it has been named the "Proust Phenomenon," after the literary example given by Marcel Proust in *Remembrances of Things Past*. In that book, the protagonist is transported to a memory of early childhood by the taste and smell of tea and cake. Scientists have studied the power of scent to awaken early memories and the findings are remarkable. Dr. Skip Rizzo at the University of Southern California has developed a virtual reality therapy for soldiers. This therapy uses visual, auditory, and even scent-based cues to trigger painful memories and then trains the soldiers to relax mind and body to overcome nervous system over-reactivity.

You will see how our basic approach to life is structured based on our memories and the reactions we had to the incidents at the time. Our sense of who we are, our positive or negative self-image and belief systems, are built on remembering ourselves in a particular way. When we change the memory, the whole personality will change.

When I say, "change the memory" I don't mean convincing a person that something did not happen or that it happened differently, but rather changing what happens when he or she thinks about the event in question. Stressful or highly charged memories demand our attention and create difficulties with normal life. If a woman has been assaulted, for instance, she may have intense frightening memories about the event. These memories may interfere with her ability to work or to interact with her family.

But even memories that are less stressful and frightening can still influence how we act, think, and feel in profound ways. Our sense of identity is based on the memories we have and the story we tell ourselves based on those memories. One of the basic strategies of positive change is to help people change the story they tell themselves about their life.

It is in the nature of the human soul to want to expand, to be free, to grow. Children express this truth abundantly in how they are naturally eager to learn, grow, play, and be unrestricted. The process of development invariably brings with it beliefs about who we are (and are not), what limits exist in the world, and what is possible for us. Yet for the people who are not content living within these mentally constructed walls, a way is needed to break free from limiting beliefs, unresolved emotions, and restrictive identities.

When you choose to make a change, something interesting happens in your life. As soon as you try to move in a new direction, you may feel nervous, insecure, frustrated, or any other of the myriad negative emotions. This is because you are running up against the inner barriers to change that you had earlier erected through experience. If you persevere, change will come.

The AFT method I will describe in this book is simply a

way to accelerate the process of change by helping to clear out limiting beliefs, feelings, and memories that are blocking the fulfillment of the natural growth pattern that we were all born to achieve.

It is my hope that you will come to understand and use the power of pure essential oils, combined with tested psychological techniques, to support emotional balance and personal transformation. If you are a practitioner, you can integrate this technique into the work you already do. If you are looking for something to use personally, try the technique yourself!

Chapter 1: The Amazing Power of Scent

The sense of smell has been identified as one of the key ingredients in a satisfying life. Whether it is the smell of food cooking, a flower garden, the perfume of someone we love, or any of a million other smells, we can gain a deep sense of comfort or joy when our sense of smell is satisfied. It has been noted that patients who have lost their sense of smell are frequently very sad.[1] In fact, a study from Virginia Commonwealth University in 2001 found that only 50% of people with an impaired sense of smell rated their life as "satisfying" compared to 87% of

---

[1] Deems DA, Doty RL, Settle RG, Moore-Gillon V, Shaman P, Mester AF, Kimmelman CP, Brightman VJ, Snow JB Jr. (1991) Smell and taste disorders, a study of 750 patients from the University of Pennsylvania Smell and Taste Center. *Arch Otolaryngol Head Neck Surg. 1991 May;117(5):*519-28.

people with a normal sense of smell.[2] According to Rachel Herz, a leader in the field of smell research, people with a disturbed sense of smell "...often report a loss of interest in normally pleasurable pursuits, feelings of sadness, loss of appetite, difficulty sleeping, loss of motivation, [and an] inability to concentrate."[3]

It has been found that the converse is also true – namely, that patients who experience bouts of sadness have a reduced sense of smell, and that their sense of smell improves once they are feeling better.[4] This is thought to occur because of the close neuronal connection between the olfactory bulb, where we detect odors, and the amygdala, where we process highly charged emotions in the brain.

Smell is a crucial component of the sense of taste, such that those without smell cannot properly be said to have normal taste any more. I remember in 4th grade doing an experiment in which we plugged our noses and then tasted either an apple or an onion. To our surprise with no smell engagement we were unable to tell the difference! Smell is involved in such daily activities as cooking, washing ourselves, cleaning our houses, and identifying those we love.

[2] Miwa T1, Furukawa M, Tsukatani T, Costanzo RM, DiNardo LJ, Reiter ER. (2001) Impact of olfactory impairment on quality of life and disability. *Arch Otolaryngol Head Neck Surg. 2001 May;127(5):*497-503.
[3] Herz, R. (2007) *The Scent of Desire*, p.4. HarperCollins
[4] Pause BM, Miranda A, Göder R, Aldenhoff JB, Ferstl R.J (2001), Reduced olfactory performance in patients with major depression. *Psychiatr Res. 2001 Sep-Oct;35(5):*271-7.

The close connection between scent and emotion is evident whenever we put a flower to our nose, or when we take a walk through a garden. We generally rate these experiences as pleasant and uplifting. Conversely, scents that we regard as disgusting or repulsive can ruin our mood, or stimulate us to feel tense or threatened.

The sense of smell is regarded as our most primitive sense. It is thought to have evolved earliest in evolutionary development. Even the simplest single-cell organisms have what is called a "chemical sense" – basically a way to detect whether what they are contacting is good for them (food) or bad for them (poison). As organisms evolved, this simple sense of good for me/bad for me became more sophisticated and turned into what we now regard as the sense of smell. It is used by higher creatures to identify food, avoid predators, attract mates, and navigate social hierarchies. For humans, vision has taken over as the primary way we assess threat and identify desired goals, but we have retained in our sense of smell an immediate and profound responsiveness, especially in emotionally charged situations.

At the level of the brain, the olfactory nerve evolved into what we now call the limbic system of the brain, the seat of emotions.

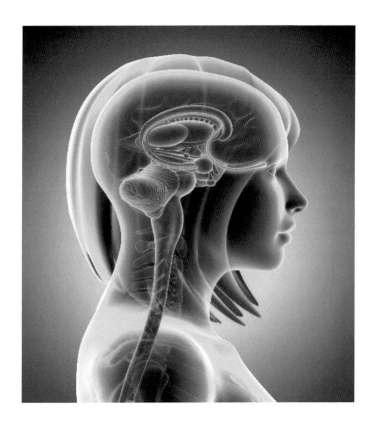

The olfactory bulb lies at the very top of the sinus cavity, and it detects odors when air rushes past it carrying aromatic molecules. It is a direct extension of the brain and extends into the limbic system, which is where we process emotion.

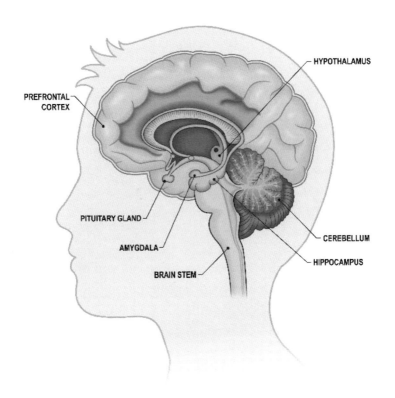

The first brain area to be stimulated is a small, almond shaped structure called the amygdala, which is the basic "fight, flight or freeze" alarm area. It is the job of the amygdala to determine in a split second whether we are in danger or not. This is critical because survival depends upon immediate detection of a predator (or prey, for that matter).

Immediately connected to the amygdala is a brain struc-ture called the hippocampus. The hippocampus is thought to be involved in the formation of memories. The hippo-campus itself can be directly stimulated by impulses com-ing from the olfactory bulb.

Reactions to smells are "auto-matic" because they are involved in very basic survival mecha-nisms. When we smell rotten food we automatically recoil, and in some cases, it even trig-gers a reflex to vomit. This makes sense. Animals need to be able to tell immediately if a food will be poisonous for them. When food has become rotten  and filled with dangerous bacteria, our sense of smell can alert our brains to initiate an impulse to move away, lose our appetite or even throw the disgusting food up. This protects us from food poisoning.

Another example is the sense of smell being used to detect predators. Prey animals such as mice and rats can use their sense of smell to detect odors related to predators in the area. Their ability to detect and avoid predators is critical to their survival. Conversely, predators use their keen sense of smell to find the prey so necessary for their survival.

Scent generated by plants can serve many purposes. In some cases, the scents act as signals. Flowers send out a sweet smell that draws insects to them, which helps ensure their survival because the insects then go on to spread the pollen to other flowers. Plants can also send out alarm scents to draw beneficial insects that come and remove the harmful insects.

It is this power of scent to act as a "signal" that we can use for enhancing our emotional life. If scent acts as a signal, and this automatically triggers responses in our brains, can we use this power intentionally to create emotional changes? Absolutely.

In one well publicized experiment, Susan Schiffman, a Psychologist at Duke University, sprayed the scent of pleasant odors such as chocolate chip cookies into New York City subway cars. The riders were found to become about 50% less likely to push, shove, and become aggressive.

Dr. Herz of Brown University has demonstrated how odors can become linked with previously unrelated emotions. In one experiment, children were exposed to an unfamiliar odor while performing a frustrating task with no solution. Later, these same children performed more poorly on a different task when they were exposed to the same odor. Their frustration had become paired with the odor, and this affected their performance and motivation. They "gave up" more easily because of the odor-induced negative mood. The ability of the odor by itself to trigger frustration has been called odor-emotional conditioning, and it has profound implications.

Suppose a child is emotionally put down and degraded by a parent repeatedly. An association will form between the presence of that parent and the feelings of shame and unworthiness. We can now consider that it is not just the presence of parent that might trigger these feelings, but even just their scent. Returning to a home that is filled with the scent of that parent might trigger these feelings even if the parent is not there.

The good news is that positive odor-emotional conditioning occurs just as frequently. We can surround ourselves with the scents that we associate with love, joy, competence, and fun. These scents can create a "garden of delight" that is supportive, strengthening, and healing. Students can condition themselves to scents and then use these scents to boost confidence and performance during test taking.

In medieval times, when hygiene was not prized, flowers and plant scents were used to make people "less offensive" to each other. Floral scents have been used as perfume to draw attention from the opposite sex. Flowers have been placed in bathing places since antiquity to encourage relaxation and healing.

Smell can signal to the brain that it is safe to relax. Researchers in Iran discovered that smelling rose oil significantly reduced amygdala firing in rats, suggesting that the essential oil protected the rats from over-excitation. Remember that the Amygdala is the structure most closely associated with the fight, flight or freeze survival mechanism. Reducing the amygdala's responsiveness would have a relaxing and stress relieving effect.

Smell is also famously able to trigger memory. We have all had the experience of smelling something that brought us back to memories from childhood. If these were happy memories, such as coming home from school and smelling cookies or fresh baked bread, we become filled with pleasant feelings. We have also experienced smelling something that reminded

23

us of a particular person – such as a cologne or cigar smell. When we smell this we have no choice but to remember – it is instant and automatic.

It is this feature of instant and irresistible triggering of memories and their associated feelings that makes the AFT process so effective.

Chapter 2: Essential Oils

Essential oils are natural extracts that are distilled from various parts of plants, such as leaves, stems, bark, flowers, roots, or seeds, depending on the type of plant used. They occur naturally in plants and function mostly as signaling molecules. Plants may use essential oils to deter predators, signal insects, initiate growth or reproductive functions, or for other reasons that we do not fully understand.

People have valued essential oils for thousands of years and there are hundreds of references to essential oils in the bible and other ancient texts. In antiquity, essential oils were used for physical healing, emotional balancing, and spiritual communion. Many religious traditions still use essential oils as part of prayer and meditation rituals, whether it be in the form of incense or resin placed in charcoal burners.

Rudolf Steiner, the Austrian philosopher and founder of Anthroposophy and Waldorf Education, stated that "Matter is most spiritual in the perfume of the plant. When the spirit most closely approaches the physical earth, then we have the perception of fragrance." He also remarked that "For every human illness, somewhere in the world exists a plant which is the cure."

In short, plants and animals have existed in co-harmony since the dawn of creation. Animals use plants for food as well as for healing, before themselves returning to the earth to be taken up again by the plant kingdom through the soil. They feed off each other in the great web of life, and are entwined physically and spiritually.

Until quite recently, essential oils have been used in Europe much more extensively than in America. Essential oils in the German language are called "Ethereal Oils" because they are thought to contain the "life force" of the plant – the "soul," that part that animates the otherwise dead matter. As much as modern materialistic medical science has rejected the concept of the soul, it cannot otherwise account for what gives life to a body. An essential oil can be thought to carry the "soul" of the plant, and it is this quality that most directly affects the human soul, or psyche. It is worth noting that the word Psychology comes from the Greek roots *Psyche* (soul) + *Logos* (Study or knowledge) and that the first Psychologists were considered "Doctors of the Soul."

The chemical constituents of essential oils are very complex – they are tiny hydrocarbon molecules. According to Dr. David Stewart, a single drop of essential oil may contain up to 40 million trillion molecules – that is 40,000,000,000,000,000,000. By comparison, the human body has roughly 100 trillion cells. This means that a single drop of oil applied to the body, if it was absorbed completely, could potentially put 40,000 molecules of oil into *each and every cell in the body*. This is why very little essential oil is needed to affect a change in the body or mind.

Each essential oil may contain dozens or even hundreds of different molecules, and it is the synergy of these components that creates the effectiveness when we use them. Chemical scientists have been able to identify and synthesize many of these molecules in the laboratory, and have been able thereby to create "synthetic oils." While these oils may have similar fragrances to the untrained nose, they may also create toxic reactions and do not possess the therapeutic benefit of a pure essential oil. They also do not possess any of the qualities of soul or energy that genuine oils have. This is why, as mentioned earlier, we only use Young Living Essential Oils with AFT, because we can be assured of their purity and their ability to retain the life force essence of the plant.

Aromatherapy as a modern discipline was initiated by French chemist Rene-Maurice Gatt---fo----say in 1910 after he experienced a dramatic healing from a very severe laboratory burn by plunging his arm into pure Lavender oil. He wrote about his nearly 30 years of research in the classic text "Aromatherapy" and thus initiated a new round of study of the composition and use of essential oils.

Essential oils were used during World War 1 for their antiseptic properties, and continued to be used until World War 2 when the use of Penicillin became widespread. His student, Dr. Jean Valnet, continued the therapeutic study of essential oils and championed their use in hospitals. To this day essential oils are used extensively in hospitals in Europe and have begun more recently to be used in American hospitals as well.

The use of essential oils for emotional conditions goes back thousands of years, and has been the realm of priests, shamans, medicine men and women, and folk-healers throughout history. In modern times, essential oils have been studied for physical healing as well as emotional balancing. We will not discuss the aspects of physical healing in this book, but readers are encouraged to look at the growing literature describing the many healing aspects of essential oils.

Emotional balancing with essential oils in the modern era is usually practiced by trained Aromatherapists, although more and more people have taken to the idea of using essential oils at home to maintain emotional wellness.

There are several main strategies for using essential oils for emotional balancing:

1. Diffusing essential oils in the home or workplace to create a calming or uplifting ambience
2. Massage with essential oils (usually diluted) to bring about a relaxation response
3. Bathing with essential oils
4. Smelling oils directly from the bottle or a cloth as needed throughout the day
5. Application of oils in an aromatherapy session
6. Dozens of other household uses

> AFT is an entirely new method of combining pure essential oils with established psychotherapy practices to enhance deep emotional release and gentle re-configuring of thoughts, feelings, and beliefs.

Essential oils can be grouped into rough categories based on the type of plant they come from and how they affect us in terms of mood.

For instance, citrus oils such as Lemon, Tangerine, or Grapefruit can be uplifting, whereas oils from trees such as Idaho Balsam Fir, Black Spruce, and Pine can be strengthening. Floral oils such as Rose and Jasmine tend to give us a feeling of sweetness whereas root oils such as Ginger and Vetiver can be grounding. Frankincense has been used for thousands of years in religious rituals because it is deeply calming. Recent research has identified specific receptors in the brain that are activated by components of Frankincense to bring about a calming effect.

Oils may also be blended to express a specific intention, such as to foster feelings of joy, hope, inspiration, or abundance. The resulting blend can be thought of as holding a particular vibration that, when smelled or applied, may assist with a particular emotional issue.

AFT uses specific blends to process negative memories, connect us to positive memories, or form associations with positive thoughts and intentions. See Appendix B for the research which supports the effectiveness of using Lavender, Vanillin, and Frankincense to balance emotions.

These are key oils in the Memory Release Blend that we use in the AFT process. We combine Young Living Stress Away™ Blend with Frankincense and Lavender, and apply it on the palms for inhalation. See the specific application instructions in Part 2 of this book.

Chapter 3: Emotional Balance

Your emotions are merely a reflection of what is happening in your life now. If you are angry it may be because you feel you have been wronged. If you are sad it may be because you have lost someone or something close to you. If you are lonely it may be because you have not found close friends or a mate. Your emotions are telling you to "solve the problem" – right the wrong, grieve the loss, make the connection.

But when your emotions are overwhelming, or when they are out of proportion to what is currently happening in your life, that is likely a sign that something from the past is being triggered.

As I had mentioned before, this book is for people who want to be free. Some people are wanting to be free from bad memories, regrets, or haunting feelings about what did or did not happen. Some people feel trapped by feelings of sadness, worry, or panic. Some people would say that they have a pretty good life, but want it to be even better. In these cases, the common denominator is something basic to human life – the desire for transcendence, the need to go beyond current circumstances and ways of being. This is a universal human need. If we want emotional balance, we can start by understanding that an emotion is our way of taking us beyond our current state.

The place of emotions in human life is often debated and frequently misunderstood. Is it good to be emotional? What about people who are too emotional? Should they just relax and calm down? And what about people who are un-emotional? Should they be more expressive?

These questions are impossible to answer unless we take a step back and define what we are talking about. Why do we have emotions in the first place? What is their purpose?

In the most basic sense, the purpose of emotions is to express our state of being so that we can get our needs met. So-called negative emotions especially should be seen as a way to communicate something that needs attention. Feelings such as anger, fear, resentment, sadness, or hopelessness all say something about how our life is going, whether well or poorly, and what we need. Emotions ideally can be expressed fully and help us reach a resolution of a painful situation.

The Cycle of Emotion

For example, to use a very simplistic scenario, let's imagine you and I are facing each other having a conversation. You come a little too close and you accidentally step on my toe. I feel pain and I say, angrily, "OW. Get off my toe!" You hear me and move back, apologizing. I say, "it's ok, don't worry." We get on with the conversation.

In this example, my expression of anger was an attempt to get a need met – namely, to get you off of my toe and to get out of pain. Because I expressed my anger directly and appropriately, you heard me and make the appropriate adjustment. When you made the adjustment and got off of my toe, I felt relieved and therefore stopped being angry, as the anger had served its function and was no longer necessary.

This is an example of a "clean" exchange of emotion and energy. After this exchange, there should be no residue of negative feelings. Remember, having feelings, even unpleasant ones such as anger or sadness, is not what causes emotional imbalance. We become unbalanced when the feelings stay with us after the event has passed and we are still holding on to what has happened.

For example, imagine that when you first stepped on my toe I did not cry out. Perhaps I felt that it is not polite to express anger or any pain at all so I just patiently waited for you to realize that you were on my toe. But you were so passionate about the conversation you did not realize that you were stepping on my toe at all. As the conversation progressed my toe hurt more and more, and I became angrier at you but still did not express it. Now I started to have more negative thoughts about you – "Why is she still stepping on my toe? What is wrong with her? Doesn't she see that she is hurting me? She must really be insensitive. I hate people like that. I can't wait to get away from such an idiotic person." When my need for relief goes unmet for so long, I begin to feel resentful.

Now a cycle of emotional imbalance has begun. I will now walk around with unresolved emotion from that exchange. Because I did not express my anger appropriately in the moment it arose, it remains circulating within me and may surface at a later, inappropriate time. Maybe a few days later I see you drop a dish and I yell at you, telling you how clumsy and inconsiderate you are. The build-up of unexpressed emotion has resurfaced but in a way that never addresses what really happened. Perhaps I make a snide remark about how I don't like people like you. Perplexed, you begin to blame me for being rude and judgmental, because you have no idea what really caused my upset.

This type of scenario is all too common in some relationships. It is the direct result of failing to allow a natural emotional expression to accomplish what it was designed to do – meet a need.

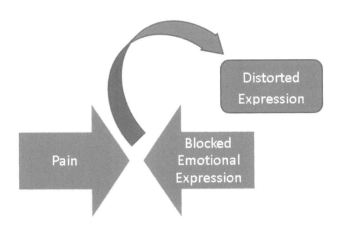

How did we get this way?

Emotional expression is hard-wired into humans (as it is for all mammals) from infancy. However, as we navigate through childhood we may experience pivotal moments in which we had an emotional reaction that we did not express for any number of reasons. When a child is abused or overpowered, the hurt, anger or sadness that she felt may not have been expressed. Or, there may be an unspoken rule in the household that she shouldn't cry. This unexpressed emotion remains within her and shapes further experiences. She may develop distrust, fear, or resentment of people based on the early experience never having been resolved. Then, when she is in a situation as an adult where there is the danger of being hurt by someone she is close to, she may react strongly – fueled by the emotion that she was unable to express as a child.

When we feel emotionally unbalanced it usually means that we are being triggered by events that are activating issues from our past. The trouble is, we often don't realize that it is the past issues that are fueling the emotion. We think that we are justified in our current emotional state. But if we express emotion in a current situation in a way that is out of proportion with what the situation calls for, it will only muddy the waters. The other person will not be able to meet our needs because we are asking for something from the past, not the present. Then they may react to our reaction, and the cycle continues.

The past continues to exist in us in the form of images, feelings, thoughts, and beliefs. Many times, these are not conscious - but they color our present experience. It is useful to draw a distinction between expressive emotion and reactive emotion. Expressive emotion is the rush of energy that arises when we have become imbalanced because a need that we currently have is not being met. It is an expression of our current state of being, and at the same time it is an attempt to get our needs met. Reactive emotion is when an unfulfilled need from the past gets triggered by a present situation that is similar in some way. It is fundamentally a distortion of current reality. A situation that is only slightly dangerous may be perceived as life-threatening, or a normal question may be interpreted as a hostile remark.

We see that emotions are primarily designed to help us

meet our needs, the most basic of which is to feel safe. When we encounter a situation that feels dangerous, we form an association between details of that event and the concept of danger. Then in the future when we encounter a situation with similar details, we are on the lookout for danger that may be coming. This is called "fear conditioning."

Let's imagine that a rabbit was out by the watering hole when it encountered a fox. The fox chased it but it was just barely able to escape. The rabbit learns from this experience that the watering hole is a dangerous place. Then, the next time he is out and about he will either avoid the watering hole altogether, or will approach it with extreme caution. The rabbit has learned something that may save its life. Thus, "fear conditioning" is a survival strategy, and if our ancestors had not been good at this, they would not have survived long enough to give birth to us.

The same holds true for situations that are not life-threatening. If a child is embarrassed in class, he may develop an aversion to school or to that particular teacher or group of students. Again, this is a survival mechanism. Although not physically in danger, he wants to avoid the painful feeling of embarrassment connected with that type of situation.

Further, the child may develop personality tendencies to protect himself. He may become introverted or may seek alternate means of compensation, such as embarrassing others to lift himself up, or become cruel to animals, for example.

Remember the cycle of emotion: Pain gives rise to emotional expression, which produces a response that leads to resolution. When the cycle is interrupted, we develop unresolved memory complexes that lead to further problems.

When there is a painful situation and the child (or adult) is unable to express and resolve the painful emotion, it remains "stuck" – in suspended animation so to speak.

When the emotional expression leads to a successful resolution, however, then there is a different type of learning that takes place. Now, in the previous example it is hard to imagine the rabbit expressing fear to the fox and the fox deciding not to chase the rabbit anymore. In that case the successful resolution was that the rabbit got away. If the rabbit were particularly thoughtful it might also draw another conclusion from the experience --namely, that it is fast enough to outrun foxes. It might develop what we call a "positive self-image."

In our human example, on the other hand, if the child could express emotionally what was going on, either to the children, a parent, or a trusted teacher, then he could also draw a positive lesson from the experience. He could have learned that even though he might experience painful emotions such as embarrassment, when he communicates how he feels and expresses it he is able to get support and to solve the problem. He might draw the conclusion that he is really "ok" and that the situation of embarrassment did not define him as a "flawed" person.

We are hard-wired to learn from our experiences, and we

form ideas and beliefs about ourselves from those experiences. For instance, a child may develop beliefs such as:

School sucks
People hate me
I am a loser

Alternately, the child may develop more positive beliefs:

I am OK
I can express who I am
People can relate to me

As children we form global judgments about ourselves. These could be positive or negative beliefs, such as:

Positive Beliefs	Negative Beliefs
I am Rich	I am Poor
I am Safe	I am in Danger
I am Strong	I am Weak
I am Smart	I am Stupid
I am Beautiful	I am Ugly
I am Confident	I am Overwhelmed

We call this whole collection of self-definitions our "self-image." Our self-image will largely determine which experiences we will seek out and which ones we will avoid. It will determine how much money we feel comfortable making and how much feels like "too much." It will determine what kind of mate we feel we can attract and what kind of house we feel ok living in.

It will determine on any given day how we approach the world – whether with confidence or with meekness.

The AFT process described later in this book will help us to re-program these limiting beliefs in order to, in effect, re-shape our subconscious beliefs to conform more closely with our consciously held goals and ideals. We need to reprogram our brain so that it can work for us rather than against us.

Chapter 4: The Nature of Memory

Our brain creates memories to organize our experiences. This is not unlike how we organize file folders on a computer. When we create a document and we save it, we need to decide which file folder it goes into. If we don't have the right folder on our computer, then we create one.

Similarly, when we have an experience we need to remember it in relation to other experiences in our life. For example, imagine you were to spend a nice day at home. That night, your brain will sift through the events of the day and assign file folders to the experience. It will put the memory of what happened that day in the "home" folder. It will also be cross-referenced with the "pleasant" folder, which contains other pleasant memories. In the future, when you think of something that happened at home you will be reminded of other memories of your home, as well as of other pleasant memories.

This is called state-dependent learning. We remember

events along with the emotional state we were in when we had the experience. Later, when we are in a particular emotional state, we will remember other events that also occurred while in that state.

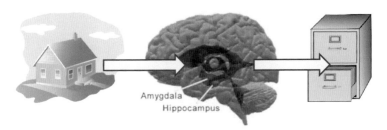

Now, however, imagine that one day you came home and found your house on fire. You were terrified. You rushed to try to save your belongings only to find yourself pushed back by the heat and smoke. You watched helplessly as everything you owned was destroyed. That night you have trouble sleeping, but when you finally do fall asleep it is fitful. You have nightmares of what happened. You awake in a panic and you have the terrifying sense of smelling smoke even though there is none present. You are haunted by images of the roof of your house collapsing in flames. You feel your heart racing and your palms sweating.

In this case, when your brain tried to process the day's events, they were too emotionally charged to fit into the file folder labeled "home," and they certainly did not fit in the file folder named "pleasant." Because they are so emotionally charged, they get kicked back to the limbic brain and re-trigger the amygdala. This activates the fight-or-flight response again and triggers you to have night-mares, intrusive memories, and panic.

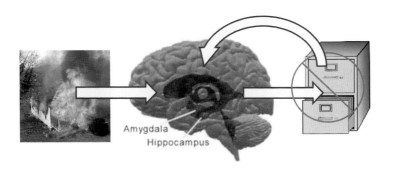

Amygdala
Hippocampus

This is the structure of what we call a "stressful memory." It is a memory that is so threatening it continues to re-trigger our survival response. It is easy to see how certain events, such as war experiences, assaults, fires, natural disasters, child abuse, etc. can become stressful memories.

How can we take a memory that is overwhelming and possibly even debilitating, and begin to make sense of it and realize that it is not still happening? One of the natural ways we do this is through dreaming. When we dream, we take pieces of what we had experienced during the day and we begin to process the thoughts and feelings triggered by those images. Researchers have found that we do this most intensely during R.E.M. (rapid-eye movement) sleep.

The first level of processing is simply to help us realize that we are not still *in* the stressful incident. We need to know that we are safe in our present circumstances. This might occur by itself with the passage of time, talking about the experience, having new positive experiences, etc.

If you have experienced a stressful incident, and if the event continues to haunt you in the form of nightmares, flashbacks, intrusive memories, and disruption of normal life, you may need additional help in processing the memory. In the next chapter, you will learn the "Memory Resolution Technique" that I developed for processing stressful memories using awareness and essential oils. If you continue to struggle with this level of distress you should seek help from a mental health professional.

Once you have completed the first level of processing and you feel safe, you can begin to re-assess residual thoughts and feelings about the event.

Returning to our example of the house fire, once you have a basic feeling of safety, you might be very focused on the experience of loss, of how you will never get to see your house again. You might curse God and think of how everything bad happens to you. You could become obsessed with safety and have trouble sleeping because you can't be sure you unplugged the hair dryer and toaster. You may even begin to think that life will never return to normal, and forget what it is like to feel hopeful, happy, and confident.

To feel better, you need to be able to draw new conclusions about the event, to cast it in a new light. In this level of processing a stressful memory, several things can happen. The positive aspects of the experience can be highlighted. For instance, you could focus on how the community came together to support you during this difficult time. You could focus on how much more precious your life seems now, or how much you love those you still get to see. You could thank God for sparing you and giving you more time on earth.

In short, we continually make *meaning* out of experiences. It is this process of making meaning that creates the transition from the shock and alarm of the original experience into what eventually become belief systems about ourselves and life.

This process of course goes on for all memories, not just stressful ones. By making meaning out of our experiences we build up our self-image, and our understanding of our place in the world. As we discussed earlier, this self-image can either be one that is empowered with positive beliefs in our gifts and abilities, or impoverished with negative beliefs and expectations about ourselves and the world.

Every experience we have becomes catalogued in this way. Even events that are not life-threatening can deeply affect our view of ourselves and the world. I remember a client I saw once who was in his 60's, who had never married and felt that he had missed out on good relationships. He related that when he was in first grade he had a crush on a popular girl in the class. The trouble is, 3 other boys also had a crush on her. Unfortunately for him, one of the other boys became her "boyfriend" and he did not "get the girl." We discussed how ever since that time he has had the belief that he is not good enough for the girls he really wants to be with. The meaning that he created from that experience influenced the rest of his life in important ways.

Using the techniques in this book, people often spontaneously report that new, positive ideas come to them once the painful memories are no longer so vivid. There is a natural movement from distress to growth, once a person feels safe.

Chapter 5: The Memory Resolution Technique

When you have a memory that has been bothering you and you can't seem to feel better about it, I suggest you try the "Memory Resolution Technique" outlined below. This process incorporates the power of scent along with specific focusing instructions on the stressful memory to support a gentle and profound re-evaluation of the memory. People find that the experience is very soothing, even when the memories they are processing are painful. I have found that this process works equally well for those whose memories are not as stressful but nonetheless disturbing and disruptive.

One of the advantages of using essential oils to disrupt the stressful memory complex is that many essential oils have been clinically shown to bring their own calming effects which can soothe the emotions even as the memory is processing. Additionally, some scents may bring positive associations. For instance, a floral smell may be soothing

47

because it brings in memories related to sweet flowers, or an evergreen scent may stimulate feelings of being in the mountains.

Since memories and the meaning we create from them are stored in our mental filing system, they can be reviewed and our response to them can be changed in some important ways.

The first step in the Memory Resolution Technique is to pull together all the aspects of the memory complex. This consists of:

1- The image or "snapshot" of what happened
2- The feeling it creates when you picture it
3- Where you feel it in your body
4- The negative thought accompanying the image
5- Any other specific details that connect with the image

In our example of the house fire, it would look like this:

IMAGE – House burning

FEELING – Terror

BODY – Heart racing, palms sweating

THOUGHT – "I am losing everything"

DETAILS – Smell of smoke, feeling of heat

Once all the aspects of the complex have been brought into consciousness, we re-process the memory by putting several drops of the *Memory Release Oil Mixture* (Lavender, Frankincense, Stress Away) into the person's hands and have them breathe the scent into all the aspects of the memory they are focusing on. It is remarkable what can happen in only a minute or two.

Below is the three-step process that I have used for years very successfully with clients when they are working with a stressful or upsetting memory.

MEMORY RESOLUTION
TECHNIQUE INSTRUCTIONS

If you want to try this process for yourself, here are the instructions. You can have a friend read these to you while you follow along, or you could even read these into a recorder and play it back so you can follow along. If you are facilitating this process for someone else, you can just read this script to them.

If there are obvious memories that are haunting you, start there. These are the memories that keep you up at night, that you find yourself obsessing about, that you feel victimized by. With this simple and gentle tool, you may quickly find yourself feeling freer than you have in years.

STEP 1

Releasing the initial memory with *Memory Release Essential Oil Mixture* (Appendix A)

"Close your eyes and picture the upsetting memory. As you picture it, get a snapshot that captures the essence of the memory. Usually a picture will automatically pop into your mind right away. As you look at this picture, notice what you feel. Find a word that captures this feeling – such as sad, terrified, nervous, confused, etc. Give it a number from 0 to 10 that represents how intense the negative feeling is, with 0 being no charge at all and 10 being the most intense possible. Now notice where you feel this in your body. It could be in your head, your chest, belly, or somewhere else. Focus on the feeling and allow it to grow in intensity. Identify the negative thought that accompanies the image. Finally, see if there are any other details of the memory that jump out at you."

"Now, when you have all of this pulled up, put a few drops of the *Memory Release Essential Oil Mixture* in your palms and slowly bring them up to your nose. As you smell the oil, imagine that you are breathing the scent of the oil in to the image, into the feeling and into the part of your body where you feel the feeling. Do this for a minute or two. Notice what happens to the image. Does it blur, move, or change? Notice what happens to the feeling. Does it change? What happens to your breathing? Does it get deeper, slower, faster? If the negative feeling intensifies, don't worry, just stay with the process. Ride the wave of emotion – don't fight it. Keep breathing the oil and soon the image will begin to fade, shift in intensity, feel farther away or changing into another memory. Keep breathing the oil until you feel the process has completed, or has gone as far as it will for now. Whatever happens is fine. You might find that the initial feeling is gone, but there is another feeling that has taken its place. That is ok, just notice what is there now. When you feel complete you can open your eyes. Now think back to the original image and notice what you feel. Give it another number from 0 to 10, ranking the intensity of the feeling you get when you picture the image."

Many times, the intensity will drop 3-6 points or even more after the first round of processing. If it has not gone down to a 0 or 1, then you can repeat the same process. It may be that you are drawn to slightly different details on each succeeding round. Keep going until you have reached a 0 or 1, or until you do it several times and it does not change any more. Then you are ready for step 2 of the process.

STEP 2

Supporting integration with *Inner Child Essential Oil Blend*

After processing upsetting memories, it is helpful to go back and reconnect with our inner core. We can do this by remembering pleasant childhood memories and returning to that feeling of innocence, purity, and possibility.

To do this, put a drop of *Inner Child Essential Oil Blend* in your palms and rub together. Then, put one palm to your nose and the other palm over your navel. Breathe the oil in, and picture a pleasant childhood memory. Let the aroma and the image transport you back to the experience, and allow yourself to feel nurtured and whole. If you are having trouble accessing a positive memory, simply go back to a time that you *wish* was positive, and imagine the event the way you wish it had been. The unconscious mind reacts powerfully to our imagination, and you may even feel the memory shifting in a positive direction simply by mentally picturing what was missing as you smell the oil.

Continue to hold your hands in the same position for a minute or two – smelling the oil from one hand and holding the other hand over your navel - and notice what occurs. Most people will feel a spontaneous shift in their mood and feel very comforted.

STEP 3

Creating a future focus with *Believe Essential Oil Blend*

After you have let go of the upsetting image and reconnected with your core self, it is helpful to anchor a positive and strong image of moving forward in a new way. This is the process of "Bringing your Best Self to Life."

Take a drop of *Believe Essential Oil Blend* and rub it in your hands. Smell the oil as you picture an image that represents strength to you. This will be a very personal image, but could be something like a strong tree, a mountain, a beloved parent or admired teacher, or a place in nature that feels sacred. Breathe that image in and feel yourself becoming one with that image. Take the strength and confidence related to that image and breathe it into yourself.

Alternatively, if there is an oil that you love deeply, breathe that oil in and picture the plant from which it came. For instance, if you love Rose oil, breathe the Rose oil in and picture yourself surrounded by roses, or holding a bouquet of roses, taking on all the qualities of a rose – beauty, love, sweetness, etc. Or if you love a tree oil such as Idaho Blue Spruce, breathe that oil in and imagine yourself in a virgin forest, surrounded by the smell and majesty of these trees, with all the qualities of strength, power, and humility that the trees represent.

Once you have done all three steps in this process notice how you feel. Notice your attitude towards the original image, as well as how you now feel about yourself and the world. There is usually a profound change and a renewed feeling of being able to get back on with living in a more open and free way.

Most people feel improvement right away, but stick with it if the memories are still impacting you negatively – there sometimes needs to be an integration period as you become used to the changes that are occurring before another layer of the stressful incidents are ready for processing.

Although this technique can be done alone, many people find it helps to have a friend sit with them as they process the memories. And of course, do not hesitate to contact a mental health professional for help with these memories if you are having difficulty. You could give him or her a copy of this book so that they will understand the technique you are using. They may even be able to help you with these techniques during your sessions.

> After Step 1 of this process, you may want to move directly into the AFT 12-step process outlined in Part 2, rather than completing Steps 2 and 3 described above. Once you have released a stressful memory, it may be helpful to set a new goal and begin working towards it. This will give your newly freed energy a direction and a focus.

Part 2: The Aroma Freedom Technique (AFT)

Introduction to AFT

Once you have mastered the Memory Resolution Technique, you have a tool you can use to reprogram areas of your life which are not working.

Our belief systems are built up throughout childhood as a result of assigning meaning to events that we live through. It is not what happens to us that makes us who we are, but rather it is more accurate to say that we make ourselves who we are through the way that we respond to the events in our lives. We literally "program" our own minds in an attempt to keep us safe.

For instance, I worked with a man named Peter who lived through his parents' divorce as a child. He had developed the belief that "nothing is stable" in life. On the one hand, this could be simply a statement of a "fact" about life. But really this was a belief that functioned as a program designed to protect him from future disappointments. By not expecting stability, he would be able to avoid the pain of being let down.

This belief that "nothing is stable" affected Peter's life in significant ways. He resisted making commitments because he did not believe that he would be able to follow through on them. He did not let himself depend on others because he anticipated that they would let him down. As such, he created a life that he just "floated through" because he lacked a solid core.

The problem with having the belief that "nothing is stable" is that it limited the kind of life he could build as an adult. He had trouble making long term plans, and he made sure that his job as a salesman allowed him to travel and move around so that he wouldn't feel stuck. Over the years this had led to emotional and financial instability.

To reprogram this belief, I asked him to find an image from childhood that captured this sense that "nothing is stable." He pictured moving to new houses several times, parents coming and going, switching schools, etc. I had him visualize it as a mini-movie, as a series of events that could have the subtitle "nothing is stable."

While watching the movie he identified the feelings of sadness, frustration, disappointment, loss, and confusion. He felt this in his body as a sense of dizziness or nausea - a "sinking" feeling.

I had Peter smell the *Memory Release Oil Mixture* in his palms for a few minutes and see what he noticed. He reported that he felt himself shaking slightly and almost being tearful as some more memories from that time flooded back. Afterwards, a kind of quietness came over him. He now felt that the statement "nothing is stable" was neither true nor false. He had de-programmed the belief.

We saw earlier how the sense of smell can unlock memories that tend to be *early* and *emotionally charged*. When a person has used the oils and gone deeply into an emotional memory, sometimes it takes a little while for the new beliefs and sense of the future to coalesce into clarity. This is not a problem. It is a state of openness that creates the space for new possibilities.

I instructed Peter that in this state of openness there are several things he could do. He could just remain in the openness of "no-belief" in relationship to those events from childhood, and allow new feelings and attitudes to coalesce over the coming hours and days. Or, he might know immediately what belief he would rather have. It could be as simple as "that happened, and I am ok." He could also have a sense of forgiving his parents and/or a peaceful acceptance of what had happened.

In this case, Peter said that he realized that to grow, he needed to set down roots. He had been hesitant to set down roots because of this previous belief that "nothing is stable." But now he felt he was ready to change that belief and live from a more empowering position. He thought about it for a minute and came up with the statement that "It is safe and rewarding to set roots down."

Then I had him stand up and take a confident, "power" posture, smell the *Believe Essential Oil Blend*, and repeat his statement for 2 minutes. I sent him home with some *Believe* oil and instructed him to do this, twice a day, for at least 3 days. In this way, he was able to re-program his subconscious mind.

Transitioning from a "Past" Focus to a "Future" Focus

The history of modern psychology began, in effect, with Freud, who demonstrated that many of his patients' adult problems came from repressed memories going back to childhood. Since his time there has been a blossoming of other approaches to dealing with human suffering, and one that emerged in the latter part of the 20th century came to be known as "Solution-Focused Therapy." Rather than looking at the past and at bad memories and problems, as Freud had done, this approach looked at the future, and oriented the patient towards what they wanted for themselves – towards solutions.

This shift in orientation was hastily embraced by some therapists while rejected by others, but in time it has become clear that a successful approach must embrace both poles of human life. If we only focus on problems we run the risk of thinking about problems all the time, and getting more of them. However, if we just focus on solutions while ignoring the sometimes very real negative patterns people are caught in, there will be no long-term growth or change.

I have created the Aroma Freedom Technique (AFT) process to embrace both aspects of life. We start by helping a person to identify what they want. Once an intention has been set, anything that conflicts with that intention will come up for healing. Each step of the process is aimed at the goal of replacing negative thoughts, beliefs, feelings, and images from a person's subconscious mind with empowering, positive beliefs and habits so that they are free to grow and progress towards the life they were meant to live.

TIP FOR USING THE AFT PROCESS

Create a safe (sacred) space – People can feel it when they are in a safe environment for self-disclosure and change. Even though the AFT process is very gentle, it can quickly access deep and sometimes long hidden memories of emotionally charged events. Therefore, we need to communicate safety and attunement when we are facilitating this process with another person.

Even if you are doing the process on yourself, it will be more effective if you do it in an environment that is free from distraction. If desired, you can smell essential oils to get clear and grounded before beginning.

Once you are familiar with the process, you can lead yourself through the steps very quickly to get yourself back on track. Keep an oil with you to smell and shift your energy wherever you are.

Remember that if you feel stuck, ask someone familiar with the process to lead you through it. And if you feel at any time that you cannot handle the emotions that you may be experiencing, consult with a mental health professional.

The 12 Steps of AFT

1. Set your goal or intention – rate how likely it seems that this goal will come to pass (0-10). Use *Clarity, Inspiration, or Highest Potential Oil Blends.*

2. Say the goal out loud and notice the first negative thought that automatically comes up – the one that tells you why this can't happen.

3. Identify how you feel when you think about the negative thoughts.

4. Notice where you feel this negative feeling in your body.

5. Drift to an earlier time, it could be recently or long ago, when you felt the same way. Find a "snapshot" or "movie" of that time.

6. Close your eyes. Focus on the snapshot, the feeling, the negative thought, and the bodily sensation while smelling the *Memory Release Essential Oil Mixture* (See Appendix A for the recipe). You may also use *Release and Inner Child Blends* for the second and third rounds if desired.

7. Allow whatever feelings surface to just pass through you as you smell the oil. Ride the wave of emotion if it gets intense. See what happens to the image and how you feel in your body.

8. Notice new beliefs starting to emerge. Find the "light" breaking through the memory. Do you get any new creative ideas?

9. Read the original goal and rate it again from (0-10)

based on how likely it seems that it will manifest. If the number is less than 8, you may return to step 2 and identify additional negative thoughts.

10. Create an affirmation that expresses the new, positive belief you wish to instill.

11. Smell *Believe or Transformation Essential Oil Blend.* Repeat the affirmation for 2 minutes with confidence, morning and night, while standing in a "power posture." Do this for at least 3 consecutive days or until you update your affirmation. Never stop doing your affirmations!

12. Make a plan, and take action daily. When you have reached your goal, set another. Find what is in your heart and pursue it!

See Easy Reference Chart at the back of the book for a quick reminder of the steps, and the Daily Affirmation Worksheet for a way to keep track of affirmations. You may photocopy those charts for personal use if desired.

Step 1: Set Your Goal or Intention

Set your goal or Intention – rate how likely it feels that this goal will be realized (0-10). Use Clarity, Inspiration, or Highest Potential Oil Blends if desired.

Setting a goal is the first step towards accomplishing anything. Before a house is built someone must set a goal and make a definitive decision to build it. Once that goal has been set, then plans can be drawn up, contractors hired, financing approved, and the actual building can be built. We need to have vision before anything can be manifested in physical reality.

If we do not set our own goals, then we will simply live out the goals and dreams of others, or drift through life without ever claiming what we really want. If I do not own my own business, I will need to work for someone else who does. If I don't want to build my own house, I will need to live in a house built by someone else.

The important thing is to decide which goals we truly want to manifest for ourselves. I believe that we all have an inner idea or vision of the life we would like to live. Many people never realize that vision because early experience has taught them what is safe and what is dangerous. We walk around trying to avoid pain, but in so doing we may be disconnecting from our path of true fulfillment.

Deep seated beliefs about religion, political viewpoints, proper ways of behaving, etc. are all imprinted into us when we are young, and may interfere with clearly seeing what we want. Layered over these are all of the beliefs about ourselves that influence what we think is possible for us in life. We create these beliefs as a way of understanding ourselves and dealing with events we encounter.

A friend of mine used to say, "Before you can get what you want, you have to know what you want." Discovering the vision in your heart may take a lifetime, but you can start by asking yourself a few leading questions, such as:

1. What would I want if money were no object?
2. What would I do if I knew I would not fail?
3. What job would I do for no money?
4. What is my heart's desire?
5. What are my special talents, gifts, and abilities?
6. What needs to be done in the world that I feel a passion to do?

Sometimes what we want is already evident to us – I want a new job, a relationship, a house, a car, to help my family, vibrant health, and so on. For any of these goals that you choose, it helps to be specific.

If you say, "I want to feel peace and love at all times," that may be too general to really mean anything. A more specific goal, for instance "being peaceful when my children are acting up" will accomplish far more, because it will trigger the reasons why you have trouble doing that. It will set in motion all of the thoughts, feelings, and memories related to what happens when they have acted up in the past, the times when you have been irritated by them, possibly some childhood memories about your own parents and how they responded when you acted up.

If you have a dream to own your own business, you might set a goal "to be fully self-employed within 1 year." Setting this goal could trigger all your fears related to leaving the security of your regular paycheck, or the fear of failure, or of what other people might think. These are the fears that have likely kept you stuck up until this point. You can use the AFT process to identify and release these fears and any associated negative beliefs that have been keeping you from moving forward in realizing your dream.

Or, you may be wondering how you can make the world a better place. You may have a specific cause that stirs you, such as concern about the environment, world hunger, economic justice or world peace. In this case, you may feel overwhelmed or not know what your role could possibly be. You could set a goal such as "I am clear about my role in _____ (your cause or issue)."

When you use the AFT process here you might identify a time in the past when you also felt confused, over-whelmed, etc. Then, once you clear this feeling using the essential oils, you may get a flash of a new idea that lets you know exactly what your next step is. I have seen this happen frequently with people – once they release a feeling that is burdening them, they become open to greater clarity and new inspirations.

Here are some examples of specific goals that could get a person's energy moving. Notice that they are written as if they have already occurred. This is powerful because it will bring the vibration of the desired reality into your brain as a thought, image, and feeling. It will also trigger your objections.

Examples:

I have a job doing _____ and paying _____ per year, starting on _____ (date).

I travel to _____ (city or country) by _____ (date).

I have achieved _____ (rank or position) in my com-pany by _____ (date), making _____ per month or year.

I am free of craving or doing _____ (detrimental habit/craving).

I am in a loving and supportive relationship.

I do what I need to do (eat well, exercise, etc.) to support vibrant health.

After setting your goal, rate it (0-10) based on how likely it seems to you that it will truly manifest. A rating of 0 means you feel totally hopeless that it could ever happen, and 10 is a feeling of absolute certainty. This will help you to assess your progress. It is not uncommon for the number to rise 1-4 points (or more) during each round of the process. We continue the rounds until we are at an 8 or higher, or there is no longer a negative voice.

There is an art to setting goals and intentions.

First, you must really want the goal that you are setting – not because someone else wants it, or because you think you should want it, or because you think it is just the best you could hope for. It must spring from your heart. It must be an expression of your true self, of a higher ideal to which you aspire.

Second, it must be something that has at least a nominal amount of rationality to it – if I say I want to get a job tomorrow that pays $1,000,000 per hour – it just isn't rational. It is out of accord with the balance of things in the universe we live in.

Third, the goal must *excite* us. When we think of it we should feel those butterfly feelings that tells us we are on the right track. Even if it feels a little scary, that is ok. In fact, if it is a little scary it means that we are pushing our comfort zone, which is right where we need to be.

Setting a goal gets us *in motion*. Just like riding a bicycle, it is very hard to remain balanced when we are standing still. But put the bike in motion and it tends to stay upright – the forward motion creates momentum and this keeps the bike from falling over. When people are emotionally unbalanced the same is true. If they feel like they are not going anywhere, their emotions will bounce all over the place. Once they have a direction that is meaningful, the emotions tend to stabilize.

Also, setting a goal should be *as much a discovery as it is a choice*. If I just choose a random goal, say, that I want to be a ballerina, this might not be the best fit for me. Sure, I could choose that goal, get the proper outfit, show up at the ballet school, and start learning to dance, but is that really what I am here to do? In my case, no. Discovering a meaningful goal is a process related to the questions we discussed above – finding what is in your heart to do – what you were *put here to do*.

There is a force in the universe that supports us when we

set meaningful goals. Once we set the goal, it often seems as if synchronicities and coincidences show up in our lives as if by magic. We may meet people who have exactly the talents we need, or we encounter opportunities that are perfect for achieving our goal. Really this is not so strange – if I have set an iron-clad goal to start building my house within one month, I will be highly focused on this and talking about it to everyone I know – this increases the chance that someone I talk to will know the perfect person to help me build it.

There is quote, attributed to German poet *Johann Wolfgang von Goethe*, that expresses this phenomenon:

> The moment one commits oneself, then Providence moves too. All sorts of things occur to help one that would never otherwise have occurred. A whole stream of events issues from the decision, raising in one's favor all manner of unforeseen incidents and meetings and material assistance, which no man could have dreamed would have come his way. Whatever you can do, or dream you can do, begin it. Boldness has genius, power, and magic in it. Begin it now.

Once you have set a goal and you say it out loud, some powerful things happen:

1. You beckon the forces of the universe to begin setting up the path to fulfillment.
2. You activate your own talents, gifts, and abilities

that support your goal and start moving you towards your goal.

3. You trigger any feelings, beliefs, or habit patterns within you that do not resonate with and support achieving your goal.

As I had mentioned, our beliefs about life have been built up based on our experiences, inherited cultural and family values, etc. These beliefs dictate what we can expect from life, and they form our self-image. If you feel called to, say, become a nurse, and you set the goal to go to nursing school, your subconscious mind will react to this information and see if there is a match between your goal and your self-image, what you believe you are.

If your goal matches your belief about yourself, then there will be no resistance to the flow of intent. You will do your studies, make applications, and anything else you need to do towards fulfilling that intention. But if your subconscious mind holds a belief contrary to your becoming a nurse, then it will block your progress. For instance, if you struggled in elementary school and developed a belief that you are not a good student, then this belief will be activated when you try to apply for nursing school – it will create anxiety, it will prompt you to make excuses about why you can't do it, it will lead to procrastination, etc. Your self-image will work to perpetuate itself.

The flow of intent is akin to turning on the water in a garden hose. The water starts flowing from the source through the length of the hose, and if there are no obstructions, it will flow freely into the garden. But the limiting beliefs are like dirt in the hose – when the water starts flowing, dirt starts coming out the other end. We try to make a change and only bad things seem to happen – this is the dirt of unresolved negative beliefs that are activated and impede the flow of water.

When the water flows freely we feel that we ourselves are "in the flow" and we are in that magical space where everything comes together to support our success.

We need to clean out the "dirt in the hose" if we want our goals to manifest. To find the dirt, you don't need to turn to extensive study of psychological theories, or undergo any painful surgical procedures. You just need to listen in to your own internal dialogue.

Some other words for "goal" here could be "intention," "desire," or even "vision." A strong intention creates a strong sense of purpose. A desire can come true when we apply ourselves in the direction of what we desire. Most importantly, when you have a vision of the life you want to lead, you can set meaningful goals that will lead you towards the realization of your vision.

Recommended Essential Oils to use in Step 1

In most cases, you do not need to use an essential oil for Step 1. The exception is when you do not feel clear about what you are wanting to create in your life. Here are some options to use:

Use *Clarity Blend* when you are trying to make a decision or don't know how to put what you are desiring into words. Put a drop in your hands, rub on your temples, and then smell your hands. Smell the oil repeatedly as you think about the goal that you want to manifest.

If you are having a hard time identifying a specific goal, you may add a drop of *Inspiration Blend* or *Highest Potential Blend* to your hand and smell the oil.

Any other oil that you find to be centering, relaxing, or inspiring can be used to create the proper mood for setting your goal or intention.

Step 2: Your Inner Voice

Say the goal out loud and notice the first negative thought that automatically comes up – the one that tells you why this can't happen.

State your goal out loud. Say what you are intending to accomplish, in detail. Say when you intend to have this done by. Then listen. Listen to the voice inside that tells you all the reasons why you *can't* have what you are intending to have. This may come in the form of seemingly rational objections, such as lack of time, money, family support, or knowledge. Or, it may come in the form of a little voice that tells you something like:

"You're stupid."

"Your parents wouldn't approve."

"You have no idea how to do that."

"You don't have enough willpower."

"You have tried that before and you failed."

Or, the negative message may come in the form of a memory or an image of a time when you failed or were humiliated.

If you truly have no internal objections come up when you state your goal, after listening for a minute, then you are probably fully aligned with it. But chances are, there will be some internal objection. This is the dirt in the hose. This voice that we hear inside has been called many things – the inner critic, the negative voice inside, the inner roommate, "stinking thinking," or the ANTs (automatic negative thoughts). There are many strategies for coping with and combating these negative thoughts, and several schools of therapy (most notably CBT – Cognitive Behavioral Therapy) have been developed with exactly that strategy.

It is helpful to understand where these thoughts come from. It turns out that these thoughts are a form of self-defense – a survival strategy. When a child goes through an experience, she learns from what happened and develops a self-image that prepares her for future encounters with the world.

This is like what happened when the rabbit barely escaped being eaten by the fox – the rabbit learned where the fox lived so that it could avoid it next time.

The child who is embarrassed at school may have developed the belief that he will be mocked when he approaches other children. He will likely develop an inner negative voice that tells him "don't do it – they will make fun of you." This negative voice is trying to protect him from the likely pain of embarrassment.

So it is with the other negative messages. The negative message that "you are too stupid to get a nursing degree" is an inner attempt to avoid the pain of failure. The negative voice saying, "my family won't support me" is trying to protect you from feelings of abandonment or betrayal. The negative message "you don't have the money," may be a rational argument based on your bank account now. Or, it could be a strategy from your subconscious mind to keep you "safe where you are."

The negative messages are there to protect us. The trouble is, they protect us by keeping us stuck where we are, versus helping us manifest a goal that would allow us to live a more satisfying life. If we want to create from a higher vision of what we want, we need to clear the dirt from the hose, to get rid of the negative messages and replace them with more empowering messages. How can we do that?

We can combat the negative messages with positive ones, as is sometimes taught when people learn to do affirmations. That is not a bad option, but as you will see if you try this, there is a constant battle between the negative and the positive voices.

Another approach is to learn to just listen to the voices without becoming attached to them. This is the path of mindfulness, and meditators have been using this strategy for thousands of years. It is a powerful strategy and I used to recommend it, but this can take years to achieve.

Or, we can go deeper inside and use the AFT process to dissolve the negative thought by releasing the emotional charge that has been holding it in place. To do this, we need to find out where the negative thought is coming from. In Step 3 we will begin to identify and clear the stuck emotional energy that is giving rise to these thoughts.

Step 3: Identify the Feelings

Identify how you feel when you think about the negative thoughts.

> This is the MOST IMPORTANT step in accessing and releasing the energy that has been holding you back. Many people fail by neglecting this step.

You have stated your goal out loud. You heard the negative message that arose. Now, pause and notice how you feel when you hear that message. If the message is telling you that you are too stupid to accomplish your goal, you might feel ashamed, sad, or depressed. If the message is a vivid memory of a time when you were humiliated, you might feel nervous that this could happen again. If the message is that you will never be able to afford your dream house, you might feel hopeless.

Remember, feelings are best expressed by a single word – keep it simple. Look for the one word that describes the feeling – mad, sad, glad, helpless, powerless, angry, frustrated, etc. If I say, "I feel like my father was mean to me when he used to ignore me all of the time," that is not a *feeling*. That is a *judgment*. If you cannot say it with one word, then you have not gone far enough in finding the feeling. Keep going until you find it – be patient. Sometimes it will be obvious, but sometimes it will not. If you get stuck, you can download a list of feelings and look at them to help you find the right word.

Pausing and noticing how you feel when you hear the message takes a moment of mindfulness. You need to become the observer, noticing the voices in your mind without getting caught up in them. It requires you to hear the objecting voice as just a statement from the subconscious mind that is trying to protect you, rather than as a directive you must obey.

Also, this step can be difficult because people tend to resist or avoid feeling unpleasant feelings. Who wants to allow themselves to feel ashamed, nervous, or helpless?

At this point, you have a choice. You can allow yourself to avoid the negative feelings through all kinds of methods – such as running to the kitchen to get something to eat, or turning on the TV to find something to distract you.

Or, you can choose to be a warrior – to courageously allow yourself to feel the pain you have been carrying, identify where it is coming from, and reach resolution in the light at the other side of the process. This technique will allow you to do that.

We do not need to get mired in the negative feeling, but we do need to touch it long enough to find out where it is coming from. Once we allow ourselves to go with the feeling, we have re-engaged the original movement of emotional energy that had gotten stuck in a previous painful experience. Once we are at this point we can complete the cycle of emotion, and become free of the negative thoughts that have been holding us back.

There is an interesting relationship between feelings and thoughts at this level:

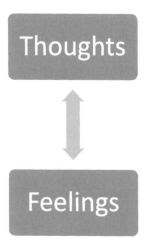

Originally, the negative feeling from an unresolved emotional process generated a negative, self-protective thought.

For instance, if you had an experience of being rejected by a group, you may have created a thought that "They don't like me. I am unacceptable. Don't approach people."

However, this thought now perpetuates itself in the sub-conscious mind as a *belief* and continually creates the feeling of inferiority and the fear of being rejected. The feeling was where the energy first got stuck, but now it is the negative belief that is keeping the painful feeling in place and inhibiting you from stepping out of your safe zone and doing what you really want to do.

Step 4: Body Awareness

Notice where you feel this negative feeling in your body.

Many people who are working on freeing themselves of negative beliefs get stuck chasing thoughts around in their head and cannot get rid of them because they are not sufficiently able to connect with the associated feelings. One way to really anchor the experience of a feeling is to notice where it is felt in the body. Every emotional experience has a physical correlate. It is not possible to be angry without tensing one's shoulders, to be scared without feeling a tightening in the belly, to be sad without a heaviness in the heart area. By focusing on the bodily correlate, we can fully experience the feeling, and this is one of the keys to helping it move.

People resist feelings because some feelings are unpleasant. Our nervous system is designed to recoil from pain. Just as we pull our hand away from a hot stove, we tend to pull away from painful emotions and feelings. For most of us, that means pulling the energy up into the head and thinking instead of feeling. Additionally, as children, before our nervous systems were mature, we have all had the experience of the *melt-down*. We have seen children who are too tired, hungry, or scared to cope with a situation just "lose it".

Because we have a memory of not being able to handle some emotions as children, we can become scared when a painful feeling comes that we won't be able to handle it and so we cut off the feeling.

Feelings are like waves, and, like waves, no feeling lasts forever. If we allow the wave to move through us, or ride the wave, it will rise in intensity, reach a peak, and then recede, leaving no trace.

If, however, we resist the emotion, we will be caught in a perpetual struggle against the wave. As it tries to move through us, we keep moving away from it, so we feel as if it is "chasing" us. If we erect a wall to keep the emotion away, it will keep crashing against the wall.

Usually a person will feel an emotion first and then they can locate it in their body. Sometimes a person cannot get in touch with their emotional state, but they can detect some discomfort in their body. In that case, I tell people to focus awareness on the bodily sensation, and this often will begin to bring the feeling to the surface.

Either way, in this step we want to locate the feeling in the body. This will help anchor our awareness on the feeling and allow us to identify where the feelings and thoughts are coming from.

Step 5: Time Travel

Drift to an earlier time, it could be recently or long ago, when you felt the same way. Find a "snapshot" of that time.

Once you have set your goal, found the negative thought, identified how this makes you feel, and located it in your body, the next step is to drift to an earlier time when you felt the same way. This is called the "feeling bridge" and we do this for an important reason.

As we learned earlier, our memories are stored in "files" composed of similar memories. Our memories are linked by association to other memories. When I remember my house, I remember lots of memories that all have my house as the common feature. The same is true with feelings. When I am in a specific feeling state, it is easier to remember other times when I had the same feeling. Since feelings are linked together in this way, a current feeling of anger, for instance, is built upon all the other times when I was angry. A current feeling of shame is built upon all the other times I felt ashamed.

So, if I have set an intention to become more visible in the world but my inner voice says something that triggers shame in me, it is hard to overcome because it is also triggering earlier, possibly more intense, feelings of shame. Shame triggers the survival response of <u>hiding</u>. When I am activating that survival response, there is no way I will want to become more visible in the world. We can see how we become at war with ourselves in this way.

We can also think of it this way: The first time we had an emotional experience, our brain planted a seed of that emotion in the soil of our brain. All later variations of that emotion are like watering that seed, which eventually grows into a big bush. If the bush is interfering with our life and  we want to get rid of it, it may not be sufficient to merely clip away a few of the leaves. We may need to dig it up by the roots.

The best way to do that is to use a "feeling bridge" and allow ourselves to drift back to an earlier time when we felt the same way – the same feeling, the same sensation in the body, possibly the same thought. It does not need to be the earliest time we can remember. It is better if we just go with the first image or memory that comes to mind. That is usually the one that will be the most effective for this process.

Here is an example. Brenda was an out of work secretary who had been having trouble finding a new job after her last job had ended poorly due to some office politics. I asked her to set a goal, and together we came up with the intention that "I will find a new job that meets all of my needs by the end of the month."

When she said this goal aloud, I asked her to notice what negative thought or memory surfaced. Immediately she began to think about failures she has had in her life, most recently because she had lost her last job. The words "I'm a failure" came into her head.

I asked what feeling went with the "I'm a failure" thought. She paused for a moment and identified that she felt ashamed.

"Where in your body do you feel the shame?"

"I feel like I have been kicked in the stomach. It makes me want to double over and fall on the ground. It takes my breath away."

"OK. Now drift to an earlier time when you felt this same feeling of being ashamed, like you have been kicked in the stomach."

Immediately she went back to a time when she was 20

years old and she was asking a family member for financial help. Instead of helping, he humiliated her.

She had just found one of the deeper roots of her current feeling of shame, one that was likely contributing to her inability to achieve her intention of finding a new job.

As we continued through the steps of the AFT process, she could let go of that earlier, emotionally charged time. She was then able to return to the present issue and felt more confidence that she could get a job.

In her case, she saw immediate results. The very next week when I spoke with her, she said that a potential employer had just called to set up an interview! Now she felt ready to embrace that new opportunity in a way she hadn't before.

It is uncanny how in almost every case, we will find an earlier, emotionally charged memory that feels similar to the current feeling. When this happens, and we release the stuck energy from that earlier experience by smelling the essential oils, a new feeling of freedom and possibility emerges.

Step 6: Smell Essential Oils

Close your eyes. Focus on the snapshot, the feeling, the negative thought, and the bodily sensation while smelling the Memory Release Essential Oil Mixture (Frankincense, Lavender, and Stress Away). For the second round use Inner Child Blend, and for the third round (if needed), try using Release Blend, especially if you are feeling "stuck" and not progressing with the memory.

After we have pulled together all the pieces of the memory complex – the negative thought, feeling, bodily sensation, and image – it is time to smell an essential oil that will allow the whole memory complex to shift.

It is important to do this preparatory work before smelling the oil. What we are doing in the AFT process is editing a memory-thought-feeling complex. If you have a file on your computer that you want to edit, you first need to pull it up into active memory and onto the screen to edit it. The same is true here. By identifying the negative complex and actively being aware of it, our nervous system can make some changes.

We saw how the sense of smell is integrally connected with the feeling and emotional sense. Something powerful happens when we smell an essential oil as we are focusing our attention on this memory complex. It is something that cannot be fully understood until one experiences it, but people describe it as "the memory just kind of washed away," or "I found it harder to think about the memory after a little while."

> Smelling the oil *disrupts* the memory complex itself. The oil stimulates a new feeling, which in a sense, displaces the previously identified feeling. Because two different feelings cannot occupy the same space at the same time, the memory complex dissolves.

What has happened is the emotional energy attached to the memory has begun to discharge. This creates a change in the experience of the memory itself – the visual details may begin to seem "farther away," or the sounds or feelings soften. Also, the meaning of the memory begins to change, and its negative effect on current life is diminished.

When all your attention is focused on heightening the feelings associated with a negative thought and a painful memory, you are intensely aware of this feeling. Then,

when you smell the essential oil, which as we recall AU-
TOMATICALLY and IMMEDIATELY induces an affec-
tive (feeling) state, it becomes impossible for the brain to
maintain focus on the memory complex.

"But," you may ask, "isn't this mere distraction? Won't
the problematic memory just return as soon as the scent is
gone?"

It would be easy to imagine that the scent has just dis-
tracted us from the painful memory, and in fact many people think that aromatherapy is only that – a temporary distraction from the real problems of life. For this reason,
aromatherapy has gained a reputation as a "lite" therapy –
pleasant enough but not deep or meaningful in helping
with our most pressing problems.

When aromatherapy is used in a casual way, to lighten the
mood or calm stressful feelings, it is true that lasting
change is harder to obtain.

But in this technique, we have done the work of drilling
down to the roots of memories that are underlying negative thoughts and attitudes affecting us today. We are introducing the scent of the oil into a deeper part of our psyche. Although it is still somewhat mysterious how this
works, people usually report that even after the scent has
been removed, they have a harder time pulling up the details of the memory, and they don't feel as strong (if any)
of a negative charge associated with the memory.

Something else happens as well. Many times, there is a
spontaneous shifting of the negative thoughts into positive
thoughts, a re-evaluation of the situation. We saw that

negative feelings often give rise to negative thoughts. Conversely, positive feelings give rise to positive thoughts. When the scent is introduced and induces a positive feeling, this positive feeling becomes paired with the memory and a positive thought can be generated from the remembered situation.

Case: Rhonda

Rhonda was a client who had been feeling sad for quite a while. She had been improving but then suffered a setback when a friend criticized her for some choices she had made. She became more withdrawn and started staying in her room all day.

We identified that an early issue of questioning her own worth had re-surfaced, so we used the AFT process. Here is the transcript of what we did:

Dr. Perkus: I want you to say the following phrase – "I'm OK with myself."

Rhonda: (after a pause) I'm OK with myself – I find it hard even to say those words.

Dr. P: When you say those words, what does the negative voice inside say to you that tells you is isn't true?

R: The voice just says, "Liar"

Dr. P: OK, when you hear the voice say "Liar," what do you feel and where do you feel it in your body?

R: I feel a bodily sensation in my shoulder.

Dr. P: OK now drift back to an earlier time when you had

that same sensation. Just say the first memory that comes up.

R: I remember being on the bus in middle school and the kids were attacking me. One of them pushed me up against the wall.

Dr. P: Smell the oil in your hands while you remember the bodily sensation and the snapshot of that time on the bus.

R: (after about 20 seconds of smelling the oil) The memory suddenly shifted and now I remember laying in the grass reading a book and eating ice chips – this is one of my favorite memories.

Dr. P: Great. Now return to the negative memory and notice what you think.

R: Now when I see it I think "I am worthy of emotionally defending myself."

Dr. P: Good and how does that feel?

R: It feels true. And a relief.

Her shift was spontaneous when smelling the oil. In this case, the essential oil may have triggered her pre-existing positive memory of the smell of tall grass (similar smells). There is no way to know what would have happened if she had smelled a different oil, but this experience is representative of what often happens with the AFT process

Recommended Essential Oils to use in Step 6

For the first round of the initial memory processing phase, we use the *Memory Release Essential Oil Mixture,* which is a combination of:

Stress Away Blend + Frankincense + Lavender

(See Appendix A)

For the second round, or if the memory was one from childhood, you may add a drop of *Inner Child Blend* to your hands and smell it to help you feel nurtured and connected to your deeper self.

For the third round, or if you feel angry, resentful, frustrated, or stuck, you may add in a drop of *Release Blend* and continue to smell the oil in your hands.

Step 7: Noticing the Changes

Allow whatever feelings that surface to just pass through you as you smell the oil. Ride the wave of emotion if it gets intense. See what happens to the image and how you feel in your body.

Everyone's experience will be slightly different when using this technique. People who are more visually oriented will notice the change in what they are seeing as the image blurs, fades, or shifts to something else. Auditory-based people will notice how what they are saying to themselves about the memory is changing. Feeling-based or kinesthetic people will feel the change in their bodies first – how the feeling or bodily sensations change. People may also feel shaking or vibrations or energy moving through their body as they smell the oil.

> The feeling may become more intense before it dissipates. Just ride the wave if the emotion intensifies. Also, keep smelling the oils. Remember that feelings are just waves and no wave lasts forever.

Another thing that can happen is the memory can trigger a different unpleasant memory, or a different aspect of the same memory. In this way, the healing process is like peeling an onion – when one layer peels away there may be another layer coming to the surface for healing. This is to be welcomed rather than avoided. Memories and events we live through are complex and multifaceted.

For instance, suppose you were dealing with a memory when you were bullied in school and the feeling was fear as you remembered the bully pushing you up against the locker. You might use the technique and move through the fear, but now begin to feel angry. Anger is a natural emotion when we are under attack, but in the original event you were too afraid to feel it. Now the anger is free to surface and be released.

If a new emotion surfaces, you may want to talk about it for a few minutes, to explore and describe it. Identify the new emotion and always find where you feel it in your body. By anchoring the next feeling in the body, it keeps you in the process. Also, find if there is a new negative thought that relates to the new feeling. In the case of anger above, it might be something like "Get away!" or "I hate you." Whatever it is, just think of it as part of the memory complex to be processed.

If you have identified a new memory complex, you can repeat the AFT process, either with the same or with a different oil. Switching oils has some advantages. Research shows that we tend to acclimate to scents fairly rapidly, so a given oil will not be noticed as much with repeated use in a single session. Also by using a new scent it gives the brain a new palette of vibrations to connect with. Just as with the case of Rhonda you never know which odors can trigger a positive memory. If you only have one oil you can use it repeatedly and will likely still gain benefit. This is because, apart from the *experience* of scent, the essential oils themselves influence mood directly through their chemical action. (See Appendix B).

Step 8: New Beliefs Emerging

Notice new beliefs starting to emerge. Find the "light" breaking through the memory. Do you get any new creative ideas?

When a person is smelling the essential oil and focusing on the memory, what is most obvious to the person is usually that the emotional charge decreases. They often also notice that the memory is fading, blurring, or shifting to something else. What also may happen is that new beliefs may spontaneously emerge.

Once the person has smelled the oil and has noticed some sort of shift, we go back and ask them how they think and feel about the memory. This will stimulate a re-appraisal of the event in question. How we think and feel about a memory is a critical component of what it means to us. In fact, the story we tell about ourselves, how we weave the memories of our lives together into a coherent whole, is the very essence of our self-esteem and self-image.

I tell people who have recently had a break-up of a romantic relationship that the story they tell themselves about why it didn't work out will have a huge impact on how they will approach future relationships and their lives. If a person feels that they were "dumped" then they will usually try to figure out why it happened – what part of themselves was unacceptable, or what they did wrong. Sometimes there are specific things one can point to – times when they should have responded with more empathy, or kindness, or understanding, etc. If this is the case, then an honest appraisal of oneself is in order – what did I learn? What can I work on doing better next time?

But more often there is just a global self-criticism – "I guess I am unlovable, or a loser, or will never find someone, or I will always push people away." It is important to realize that this self-criticism is a story the person is weaving about themselves, and that the story can be changed.

In the case of a break-up, we might work on the memory of when they heard the news of the break-up (where they were, how it happened). In working with this memory there will likely be some negative thoughts that come up. After processing the memory, we will see how they feel and think. If the feeling is not so intense any more, we may need to help them formulate a new appraisal of the situation, such as:

"I accept what happened and now I can let go of _____ (the person)."

"I forgive myself and _____ (the person) for the relationship not working out."

"With what I have learned from this experience I know that my next relationship will be better."

Whatever the issue was, we want to be able to have a positive appraisal of the event. In many cases, it is not realistic to think positively about a significant loss, but in these cases a person can still develop a healthy attitude about that loss, such as:

"I am finding new ways to enjoy life."

"I am making my life meaningful even though I have lost _____ (person)."

"I am growing more peaceful every day."

When you are using the AFT process, you want to be actively *looking* for a positive belief to emerge from the ashes of the dissolving memory complex. When you do this, you are taking ownership of your life and choosing to take yourself in a new direction. Don't *pretend* to believe a positive thought if you are still stuck in negativity, but rather, look for the opening, the ray of light you can find that shows you a way out of the previously stuck attitude.

Step 9: Revisiting Your Goal or Intention

Read the original goal or intention and rate it again (0-10) based on how likely it seems that it will manifest. If the number is less than an 8, return to step 2 and identify additional negative thoughts. Even at an 8 or 9, ask if there is anything else the negative voice is saying. If there is still a negative voice, return to step 2.

Here is where we see if the procedure has accomplished what we set out to do. Remember that the original idea was to free ourselves up so that we could reach our goal. By identifying and clearing out negative beliefs, feelings and memories, the energy should be flowing more freely now in the direction we had intended.

Say the original statement of intent again and give it a rating (0-10) based on how likely it seems that the goal will manifest. If there has been a change, the feeling now should be more confident. Also, after saying it, the little voice inside your head should be quieter. It either has nothing negative to say, or it may even say something positive, such as "I know I can do this!"

Try it and see what you notice.

For some people, it is hard to even say the original goal or intention at all in the beginning, and afterwards they can say it with ease.

At this point, there may be different concerns, worries, or negative thoughts that surface when saying the intention again. If that is the case, you can go back to Step 2 and repeat the whole procedure using the newly discovered objections. After all, each round only takes a few minutes. Doing several rounds of clearing is not a problem.

For instance, at the beginning the rating might be a 3, and it rises to an 8 afterwards. Occasionally your number will go down at first. If that happens, do not despair! This just means that you have tapped into a deeper memory complex that is now ready to be released. Stick with the process and you will soon feel better than ever!

If it is not a 10 afterwards, it may be because there are other emotionally laden internal objections, in which case you can go back to Step 2 and clear another layer. Or, your voice may be telling you that there are external action steps (applying to the school, hiring the architect, getting your business license) that need to be addressed before reaching a rating of 10.

Step 10: New Outlook, New Attitude

Create an affirmation that expresses the new, positive belief and attitude you wish to instill.

Once you are feeling good about your stated goal, and you have cleared away the negative thoughts and feelings that may have been inhibiting your energy, it is critical to anchor this feeling by creating an affirmation describing your soon-to-be-realized new reality. Researchers have found that positive self-affirmations help improve problem-solving ability among people who have been chronically stressed.[5]

Most people have heard about affirmations but there is

---

[5] Creswell JD, Dutcher JM, Klein WMP, Harris PR, Levine JM (2013) Self-Affirmation Improves Problem-Solving under Stress. *PLoS ONE 8(5): e62593. doi: 10.1371/journal.pone.0062593*

still some confusion about how to properly use them.

An affirmation is a statement, written in the present tense, that describes the reality you desire to have even though it has not manifested yet. It could be descriptive of a specific situation, such as "I now have a job that I love that pays me $100,000 a year." Or, it could be describing an emotional situation, such as "I feel loved and welcomed wherever I go."

By saying the affirmation several times, morning and night, or even all day long, it will gradually sink in and we will start to believe it and act from that place. Affirmations can be powerful, but there are couple of things that make them work much better.

First, we need to clear out the beliefs, feelings, and attitudes that are in direct conflict with the affirmation. This is exactly the purpose of the AFT process. By starting with the statement of our goal and listening for the negative voice, we are identifying attitudes that are not in alignment with that goal. Then we find the feelings and memories underlying the negative voice and its objections. Smelling the essential oil helps to re-configure the memory complex and remove the emotional charge behind our objections. Once this inner resistance has been overcome, our mind will be more receptive to the new goal.

Second, we need to understand that when we are saying the affirmation, we are not trying to argue with our assessment of reality now. If I say "I now have a job that I love that pays me $100,000 a year" and my logical mind knows that is false, it will create an internal state of confusion and resistance.

Remind yourself that the purpose of saying the affirmation is to *program* your subconscious mind. It is all right if your logical mind knows that you are currently unemployed. You are not trying to convince yourself that you have that great job. Rather, you are creating a feeling of being *open* to having that job, and acting *as though* it were already true. Repeating this daily makes the feeling not seem so strange.

Affirmations are important because they give our mind direction. Every day when we wake up it is a new day, and our usual tendency is to just approach the day based on however we are feeling – excited if there are fun things scheduled, serious if we have tasks to do, or with dread if we have unpleasant things on our mind. By having an affirmation that was created during a time of *clarity* – we can continue these insights and bring them into the times when we may have forgotten our new chosen direction.

Examples of good affirmations:

"I am productive and focused today."

"I learn easily and remember what I have learned."

"I am a thoughtful and considerate husband."

"I am peaceful and kind throughout the day."

"I choose to be radiant even when others are being negative."

Remember your affirmation must be in the present tense,

and describe a positive quality you want to exhibit, rather than a negative quality you wish to avoid. It has been said that the subconscious mind does not register the word "not" – try to *not* think of a pink elephant, and right away you will. To put it another way, if you go to Paris and ask the taxi driver to *not* take you to the Eiffel Tower, he or she will still have no idea where you want to go. The same is true in our lives – becoming clear about, and affirming, what we want will get us there much more quickly than simply trying to *avoid* what we do not want.

To find a good affirmation organically, you can ask "what is the positive voice saying now?" Sometimes you have already heard the voice say something like "You got this," or "Be open to change," or "It is time to let go," etc.

This is your inner wisdom speaking. Once you clear out the negative voices it is much easier to hear the positive, guiding voice within.

Some people describe this as their intuition, their logical mind, or even the Holy Spirit. In fact, those who have a biblical foundation may have a scriptural verse come such as "I can do all things through Christ who strengthens me."

Whatever you have spontaneously heard during the clearing is the right affirmation for you.

Step 11: Anchoring Your New Reality

Smell Believe or Transformation Essential Oil Blend. Repeat the affirmation for 2 minutes, with confidence, morning and night, while standing in a "power posture."

Research has shown that odor-conditioning can affect motivation.[6] Subjects who worked on a frustrating puzzle in the presence of an ambient odor were later quicker to give up on a task when they were exposed to the same odor, compared to those who had not been conditioned to associate frustration to the odor. Dr. Rachel Herz of Brown University has contributed greatly to research in this area and has summarized the possibilities as follows:

---

[6] Olfaction, emotion and associative learning: Effects on motivated behavior (2004). *Motivation and Emotion*, 28, 363-383. Herz, R.S., Schankler, C. & Beland, S.

By linking feelings of intellectual competence to a specific odor and then using this odor when confronted with challenges at work or school, odor-emotional conditioning could be used to improve performance and productivity among individuals with low scholastic or job morale.[7]

We will be using this principle to our advantage when anchoring our new desired reality with affirmations. By saying the affirmation while smelling an essential oil, we create a link between the positive emotion, positive belief, and the aroma of the oil. In the future when we smell the oil it will help to induce these same feelings and mental states.

There is an integral relationship between mental states and the body. In an earlier step, we learned that finding the negative emotion in the body helped us to become more aware of the feeling and it deepened the process of re-patterning the memory complex.

The relationship between mind and body goes both ways. We will see that body states have a profound impact on mental states as well. Amy Cuddy of Harvard University has demonstrated that having people assume "power postures" for as little as 2 minutes significantly improved confidence and reduced stress.

In that research, subjects were asked to assume either a "power" pose (standing erect with shoulders back and chest out, arms to the side, feet wider than hips) or a "weak" pose (standing or sitting with arms crossed, chest

---

[7] Herz, R. (2007) *The Scent of Desire*, p.12. HarperCollins

caved in). Then, they prepared for a mock job interview while in one of the two pose categories (power or weak). Independent raters overwhelmingly said they would choose the subjects that had prepared with the "power pose" for the job, even though they did not know which postures the subjects had been holding while preparing for the interview.

Additionally, she tested the saliva of volunteers before and after using the power postures, and found that even biological markers significantly improved. Subjects had an increase in testosterone, which is associated with self-confidence and assertiveness, as well as a decrease in cortisol, which is a marker of stress levels. Lowered cortisol indicates a reduction in the physiological stress response.[8]

[8]Cuddy, Amy J.C., Caroline A. Wilmuth, and Dana R. Carney. "The Benefit of Power Posing Before a High-Stakes Social Evaluation." Harvard Business School Working Paper, No. 13-027, September 2012. Additionally, I recommend her TED talk at:

Standing in a "power posture" primes us for success both mentally and physiologically. When we combine this with affirmations and smelling essential oils, we create an extremely effective way to shift our whole attitude and approach to life. We are programming ourselves for success every day.

My recommendation is to say the affirmation, with confidence, for 2 minutes in the morning and at night, while smelling the oil and standing in your "power posture."

In the succeeding days as you say the affirmation, there may be some times when it feels true and right. However, there may be times when you say the affirmation and right away you hear an objection from your inner voice. Keep going. Saying the affirmation, smelling the oils, and standing in the power posture should place you into a more

https://www.ted.com/talks/amy_cuddy_your_body_language_shapes_who_you_are?language=en

positive state of mind.

A power pose can be a confident, hands on hips pose, as if to say, "I am ready to meet the day." Or, it could be an "openness to receiving" pose. One woman I worked with was releasing her emotional blocks to having a loving relationship. When it came time to do the affirmation, the most appropriate posture seemed to be one with arms outstretched, welcoming her future partner into her life. This posture can also be used if you need to let someone or something go.

If after doing the affirmation you are still feeling unsure about your alignment with the affirmation, take a few minutes and go back to the beginning of the AFT process. Restate your original goal and follow through the steps.

It is not uncommon for additional objections, negative beliefs, fears, or feelings to surface as the days go by. We all have "good" days and "bad" days. When you are having a bad day, it is a perfect time to release the negative programming that may be interfering with your outlook. Additionally, each step we take towards greater well-being and success in our lives brings the possibility of deeper objections being raised from our subconscious mind. As stated in the Introduction, these objections are an effort of your subconscious mind to protect you. You may have experienced pain in the past when you tried something new, or tried to reach a goal, or expressed joy, for instance. Now, as you reach towards your new goal and desired life, there may still be a part of you that fears that something bad might happen again. Therefore, look at these objections as an opportunity to grow past your existing limitations.

Saying an affirmation for several days in a row will program it in to your subconscious mind. If, during that time, you find that your goal is changing and evolving slightly, it is ok to create a new goal or affirmation. The most important thing is consistent application of the method.

Don't stop!

The day you stop re-programming your subconscious mind with intention and affirmations is the day your old programming has a chance to creep back in and interfere with your progress.

Step 12: Putting It All into Action

Make a plan, and take action daily!

You must now take action in order to realize your goal. Everything we have talked about and done so far will not come to much if you don't. You may be saying wonderful affirmations about living in a mansion, but if you do not create a plan and take action, you may end up with your house being re-possessed!

We spoke earlier about how our subconscious memory complexes, to protect us, act to block our intentions just like dirt will block the flow of water in a hose. Once we have "cleaned the dirt out of the hose" using the AFT process, and have the power of intent flowing through us, we need to create a plan of action.

I like to sit quietly for a few moments after saying my affirmation and notice what creative ideas come to me for fulfilling my intention. You may be surprised at how easily the ideas flow once you have eliminated your inner resistance. Saying your affirmation with the oils and power posture places you in a very receptive mental state, in which the thoughts and ideas that come to you may be particularly relevant. If a person pops into your mind at that moment, call them immediately. You may find that they have a clue or resource that you need.

Sometimes it is not clear what positive actions will bring the result you want. If you want to find a mate there is no magic formula of how many dates you need to go on, or people you need to meet. But recognize that when you activate the power of intent, a way is being cleared to the realization of that intent. You need to listen to inner promptings that may be "putting you in the right place at the right time."

Have a note-taking device handy – paper, computer, phone, etc. – and get your ideas down. Then sort through them to determine which of them are the ones to accomplish *today*. Others can be organized by a timeline that makes sense for them. For instance, you may get a creative idea to make a presentation for a local group, but the group doesn't meet today. So, you need to put "contact local group" on your list.

As the days go by keep adding to your list. After your daily affirmation, when you glance at the list you may get a feeling about which is the most important item for today. Decide to do it right away. You will feel so much better when you are taking decisive action towards your dreams. Remember, as Goethe said, "Boldness has genius, power, and magic in it."

You might create a plan to write a book by a certain date, and realize that this is only possible if you write 10 pages a day, or for 4 hours a day, or whatever it is. Once you figure this out, you need to put in the work. This is a dynamic process. When you have done some work towards your goal this will create a new energy that you bring to the next day's affirmation. The project will evolve so it is important to check in daily to determine that you are still going in the direction that is right for you.

Be honest with yourself about how you feel the process is going. If you are getting discouraged, don't give up – all it means is that there is additional work to do in identifying what your doubts are, what your inner voice is saying. Realize that these are either:

1. Negative thoughts coming from your subconscious mental programming, or
2. New information that you need to integrate into your ongoing manifestation process.

If they are negative thoughts such as "This will never work, I can't do it, nobody will be interested," etc., these are most likely mental programs that at one time served you, but now are only keeping you stuck. Use the AFT process to clear these subconscious objections out and then keep going with your affirmations.

However, sometimes as a project progresses we get valid information that changes how we think about it. We may realize that our original goal was not *exactly* what we wanted, or that from our new perspective we want something slightly different. This is to be expected and welcomed.

For instance, suppose you initially had set a goal to build your dream house on 20 acres with horse paddocks in exactly one year's time. Along the way, however, you got a new job in a different city and realized that you enjoyed living in the downtown environment. You wouldn't keep affirming your *old* dream – that would not make any sense. In this case, you would work on new goals that are more aligned with your current life situation.

Be alert for surprising new insights and developments that put you in an even *better* situation than you had originally envisioned. "This or something better now manifests" is a good addition to any affirmation.

Every day when you take action, write down or check off on your to-do list what you accomplished towards reaching your goal that day. Seeing all you have done as the days go by helps to reinforce that you are moving in the right direction.

Conclusion

We saw earlier in this book how the sense of smell can immediately and powerfully modify our moods and emotions, and how this can affect motivation and learning. Further, our emotional balance can be disrupted by unresolved memories, thoughts, and feelings from earlier experiences. We used the example of stressful memories to show how we can disrupt these memory complexes with essential oils by smelling them at the right time in the process. In this way, painful memories can become integrated and the negative thoughts related to them can be transformed into less distressing or even positive thoughts.

This process set the stage for using essential oils as part of a new technique for overcoming our inner resistance and realizing our deepest desires for living a fulfilling life. The Aroma Freedom Technique is a way to quickly identify and let go of thoughts and feelings that are not in alignment with our heartfelt intentions.

To review the 12-Step process:

The first step (optional) is to use *Clarity, Inspiration, or Highest Potential Essential Oil Blends* to help you get clear about your goal, desire, or vision. Choose an intention that comes from your heart, is exciting to you, and maybe feels just a little out of reach. This will activate any thoughts or feelings that may be keeping you stuck. Rate your goal (0-10) based on how likely it seems that the intention will manifest.

Then, identify the negative thought that pops up when you state your goal. There may be several negative thoughts but usually the first one is the one immediately blocking your goal. Notice how you feel when you say the negative thought, and where you feel it in your body. Then, you drift back to an earlier memory, either recently or long ago, when you felt the same way. Now, see the "snapshot" or "movie" of that memory, pay attention to the feeling and the negative thoughts, and smell the *Memory Release Essential Oil Mixture* (Lavender, Frankincense, and Stress Away).

As the memory shifts, become aware of new, positive thoughts that may emerge. Say your goal again and rate it (0-10) based on how likely it seems that it will manifest. If it is not above an 8, go back and identify another negative thought, and repeat the process. Even at an 8 or 9 you can still ask if there is anything else the negative voice is saying.

Once you are feeling sufficiently positive about your goal coming true, identify an affirmation that expresses the new reality you are choosing to move into. Say it with a "power posture" or a "receiving posture" while smelling *Believe or Transformation Essential Oil Blend.* Write your affirmation and say it for 2 minutes, morning and night, for at least 3 days, or until you create a new affirmation.

You must remember that your subconscious mind will be guiding you based on the programming that is currently active. Keep programming your mind daily using the AFT process. If you do not do this, you may revert to earlier, no longer relevant programming that is designed to keep you where you are, rather than helping you to move forward.

> Using the AFT process daily (whether creating a new goal or strengthening an existing one) helps you to remain focused on the steps you need to do every day as part of realizing your dreams and living a rewarding, meaningful life.

The process is not designed to be a form of psychotherapy in and of itself. Rather, it is a process that can be integrated with other approaches or used on its own as a quick way to achieve a "course correction" and to give energy to any goal you may be seeking.

The AFT process is a safe, simple, and quick method to restore emotional balance and to activate intentions. I have found it to be extremely helpful in my own life, to get me back on track when I start to falter on a project or a goal. I have used the various elements of the process, such as setting goals, identifying negative thoughts or feelings, shifting memory complexes with essential oils, and using affirmations, for many years.

The current form of the process that is now known at the Aroma Freedom Technique (AFT) is an integration of these various parts into a coherent whole. Although once you learn and try the technique you will find that it only takes minutes, it is built upon a series of steps that have emerged following the advances gained by a century of practice and research by psychotherapists in the field. When we integrate the dimensions of thought, feeling, bodily experience, and aromatherapy, the results can be remarkable. It is my hope that you will use it regularly and that your life will become all that you want it to be!

I encourage you to use AFT on friends, family, and colleagues just by using the steps outlined in this book. However, if you would like to use AFT in a clinical setting (psychotherapy, massage, etc.) then you are required to become a certified practitioner. You can find more information about becoming certified at www.drperkus.com.

Your future is only limited by what you can imagine, and what you believe yourself to be. Find what is in your heart, pursue it with passion, and live the life of your dreams!

Appendix A

The blends referred to in this book have been created by Dr. Gary Young, founder of Young Living Essential Oils. According to his own accounts, when he formulates a blend, he first sets an intention for what he wants to accomplish with the blend. He then considers the energy of each oil along with what is known scientifically about it. Finally, he goes into a state of prayer and receptivity to find the final recipe. Many times, this is a quick process, but sometimes it may take months for the information to come together to create the desired blend.

Selected Young Living Blends referred to in this book contain the following single oils:

Believe - Idaho Balsam Fir, Coriander, Bergamot, Frankincense, Idaho Blue Spruce, Ylang Ylang, and Geranium essential oils.

Clarity – Basil, Cardamom, Rosemary, Peppermint, Coriander, Geranium, Bergamot, Lemon, Ylang Ylang, Jasmine, Roman Chamomile, and Palmarosa essential oils.

Highest Potential - Australian Blu [a blend of blue cypress, ylang ylang, cedarwood, blue tansy, and white fir], Gathering essential oil blend [galbanum, frankincense, sandalwood, lavender, cinnamon, rose, spruce, geranium and ylang ylang], jasmine and ylang ylang.

Inner Child - Orange, Tangerine, Ylang Ylang, Sandalwood, Jasmine, Lemongrass, Spruce, and Neroli essential oils.

Inspiration – Cedarwood, Spruce, Myrtle, Coriander, Sandalwood, Frankincense, Bergamot, Spikenard, Vetiver, Ylang Ylang, and Geranium essential oils.

Release – Ylang Ylang, Olive oil, Lavandin, Geranium, Sandalwood, Grapefruit, Tangerine, Spearmint, Lemon, Blue Cypress, Davana, Kaffir Lime, Ocotea, Jasmine, Matricaria, Blue Tansy, and Rose essential oils.

Stress Away – Copaiba, Lime, Cedarwood, Vanilla, Ocotea, and Lavender essential oils.

Transformation - Lemon, Peppermint, Sandalwood, Clary Sage, Sacred Frankincense, Idaho Blue Spruce, Cardamom, Ocotea, and Palo Santo essential oils.

Memory Release Essential Oil Mixture:

Blend equal parts **Stress Away, Frankincense, and Lavender.** Or, put one drop of each oil in palms and smell.

A note on the essential oils discussed in this book:

I am a Clinical Psychologist and have been using Young Living Essential Oils in my private practice for over 15 years. The Young Living Oils are very high quality. I have personally visited some of the farms and laboratories owned by the company, and I have a great deal of respect for their high standards and production processes. I recommend only using oils from Young Living for the techniques described in this book.

Some of the oils discussed in this book are blends. I have included a list of single oils that are part of the blends earlier in this Appendix, so that you can experiment with some of the single oils contained in those blends, or even different blends altogether. AFT is a very flexible technique and you may get satisfactory results when you substitute one oil for another. If you are not getting the result you want, though, it may mean you need to try the exact oils I am recommending.

You can purchase the recommended oils from the person who gave you this book, or at
www.drperkus.com.

Appendix B

Selected research on the effectiveness of essential oil constituents on mood

Lavender:

In 2010 Researchers in Germany studied the effectiveness of Lavender oil in capsules and found it to be as effective as Valium for the treatment of Generalized Anxiety Disorder.

Reference: Woelk H, Schläfke S. (2010) A multi-center, double-blind, randomised study of the Lavender oil preparation Silexan in comparison to Lorazepam for generalized anxiety disorder. *Phytomedicine. 2010 Feb;17(2):94-9. doi: 10.1016/j.phymed.2009.10.006. Epub 2009 Dec 3.*

Vanilla:

In 2015, Researchers in China found that Vanillin (the key aromatic component found in Vanilla) could alleviate depressive symptoms in rats via the olfactory pathway. They demonstrated that Vanillin increased both Seratonin and Dopamine levels in the brain tissue.

Reference: Xu J, Xu H, Liu Y, He H, Li G. (2015) Vanillin-induced amelioration of depression-like behaviors in rats by modulating monoamine neurotransmitters in the brain. *Psychiatry Res. 2015 Feb 28;225(3):509-14. doi: 10.1016/j.psychres.2014.11.056. Epub 2014 Dec 9.*

Frankincense:

Researchers at Hebrew University in 2008 discovered that Incensole Acetate, a component of Frankincense, acts on specific receptors in the brain that lead to an anti-depressant and anxiolytic effect.

Reference: Moussaieff, A., Rimmerman, N., Bregman, T., Straiker, A., Felder, C. C., Shoham, S., ... Mechoulam, R. (2008). Incensole acetate, an incense component, elicits psychoactivity by activating TRPV3 channels in the brain. *The FASEB Journal, 22*(8), 3024–3034. http://doi.org/10.1096/fj.07-101865

AFT Quick Reference Guide

1
- Set Your Goal. Rate its likelihood (0-10). Smell *Clarity, Inspiration, or Highest Potential* if desired.

2
- Listen for the negative voice that tells you this can't happen.

3
- Identify how you feel when you hear the negative voice.

4
- Find where you feel the negative feeling in your body.

5
- Drift back to an earlier time when you felt the same way, either recently or long ago.

6
- Smell *Memory Release Mixture* while focusing on thought, feeling, and memory.

7 • See what happens to the image, thoughts, and feelings. Use *Inner Child or Release Oil* if desired.

8 • Notice new beliefs starting to emerge. Identify creative ideas related to your goal.

9 • State your original goal aloud. Rate it (0-10). Return to step 2 if less than 8.

10 • Create an affirmation that expresses your new, positive belief.

11 • Say the affirmation, smell *Believe or Transformation* oils, stand in Power Pose (2 min, 2x/day).

12 • Make a plan and take action daily. Listen for new guidance and update intentions.

AFT Affirmation Worksheet

Affirmation:

_____

_____

_____

Repeat the affirmation for 2 minutes, twice per day, with conviction while standing in a power pose. Smell *Believe or Transformation Oil Blend* as you do this.

Repeat for *at least three consecutive days,* or until you create a new affirmation. Check off each box when complete.

Always make sure that your energy feels clear when you say the statement. If you experience inner resistance, use the AFT process to identify and release any negative thoughts, feelings, or memories that come up.

Date	AM	PM

Next Affirmation:

_____

_____

_____

Notes/Inspirations:

_____

_____

_____

_____

_____

_____

Program your mind daily!

As soon as one affirmation is complete or the goal has been reached, create another. Make affirmations a daily habit and soon you will not feel right unless you have done your daily practice. This will keep you focused in the direction of your dreams.

Feel free to experiment with different oils as you progress.

About the Author:

Dr. Perkus is a sought-after speaker and trainer who inspires people all over the world to make life changes using essential oils and positive psychological processes. He received his bachelor's degree in Philosophy from Binghamton University (Phi Beta Kappa) and his doctorate in Clinical Psychology from Duquesne University. He has drawn on over 20 years of clinical experience to develop unique methods that help people to overcome their inner resistance and to realize their dreams. His work bridges the fields of psychotherapy and aromatherapy. He is considered an authority on how to clear emotional blocks with essential oils, and he speaks internationally on the topic. He is the creator of The Aroma Freedom Technique, and he helps individuals, groups, and institutions learn how to boost happiness and productivity by using AFT.

To inquire about trainings or speaking engagements he may be reached at www.drperkus.com.